WINNIPEG
JAN 0 6 2012
PUBLIC LIBRARY
WITHDRAWN

CAKE BASICS

D0557186

A FIREFLY BOOK

Published by Firefly Books Ltd. 2011

Copyright © 2011 Marabout

All rights reserved. No part of this publication may be reproduced, stored in a retrieval system, or transmitted in any form or by any means, electronic, mechanical, photocopying, recording or otherwise, without the prior written permission of the Publisher.

First printing

Publisher Cataloging-in-Publication Data (U.S.)
Fawcett, Abi.
   Cake basics : 70 recipes illustrated step by step / Abi Fawcett ; photographs by Deirdre Rooney.
[256] p. : col. photos. ; cm.
Includes index.
Summary: A photographic, step-by-step guide to basic cake baking skills and techniques.
ISBN-13: 978-1-55407-940-7 (pbk.)
1. Cake. I. Rooney, Deirdre. II. Title.
641.8/653 dc22   TX771.F393   2011

Library and Archives Canada Cataloguing in Publication
Fawcett, Abi
   Cake basics : 70 recipes illustrated step by step / Abi Fawcett; photographs by Deirdre Rooney.
(My cooking class)
Includes index.
Translation of: Les gateaux maison.
ISBN 978-1-55407-940-7
   1. Cake. 2. Cookbooks. I. Rooney, Deirdre II. Title. III. Series:
My cooking class
TX771.F3913 2011   641.8'653   C2011-901601-X

Published in the United States by
Firefly Books (U.S.) Inc.
P.O. Box 1338, Ellicott Station
Buffalo, New York 14205

Published in Canada by
Firefly Books Ltd.
66 Leek Crescent
Richmond Hill, Ontario L4B 1H1

Printed in Canada

MY COOKING CLASS

CAKE
BASICS

70 RECIPES
ILLUSTRATED STEP BY STEP

ABI FAWCETT
PHOTOGRAPHS BY DEIRDRE ROONEY

❋ ❋ ❋

FIREFLY BOOKS

INTRODUCTION

~~~~~~

What makes a good cake?

For me it's all about the texture and flavor. A dry cake can be such a letdown. Good dishes require great flavors, and for cakes it's no different, whether it's vanilla, chocolate, cheesecake or citrus.

I have been in love with making cakes for as long as I can remember. My friend Danni and I used to turn my mom's kitchen upside down in pursuit of the perfect cake! Later, I put this passion to work as a chef in the pastry section of a busy London restaurant, where my great joy was inventing cakes.

Cake baking is above all a pleasure: making discoveries, trying out new recipes and finding new flavors. Sometimes it can be disappointing, but I hope that this book will answer some of the questions you may come across, such as, why has my cake sunk? One such problem I have encountered along the way is the temperamental nature of ovens. A simple solution to this problem is to buy an oven thermometer, which can make all the difference to your cake.

I do hope that this book will help you find many of your favorite recipes, such as the classic fruit cake, Victoria sponge cake and cherry and almond cake, as well as some new ones that I know you'll love. The salted caramel cake is an all-time favorite of mine.

I have also included some menus at the back to give you ideas for the cakes you can serve when you are planning a girls' night in or an afternoon tea party.

So get your baking gear together, put on your apron and let's bake cakes!

✳ ✳ ✳

CONTENTS

BASICS

1

WHAT YOU NEED & TROUBLESHOOTING

ICINGS & FROSTINGS

DECORATIONS

EQUIPMENT

1. **Whisk:** for whisking. 2. **Wooden spoon:** for mixing. 3. **Skewer:** to test if cake is cooked 4. **Palette knife:** for spreading icings. 5. **Spatula:** for mixing and folding in. 6. **Metal spoon:** for mixing and folding in. 7. **Microplane grater:** for grating citrus zest. 8. **Parchment paper:** for lining pans. 9. **Wire rack:** for cooling cakes. 10. **Bundt pan.** 11. **Loaf pan.** 12. **Oven thermometer:** to check oven temperature.

13. **Round cake pan.** 14. **Hand-held electric mixer:** for mixing and whisking 15. **Stand mixer:** makes mixing and whisking easier. 16. **Food processor:** for chopping and mixing. 17. **Food processor (small):** for chopping. 18. **Marble block:** good for spreading out chocolate for curls. 19. **Chopping board:** for chopping. 20. **Grater:** for grating. 21. **Rimmed baking sheet:** for baking.

INGREDIENTS

1. Eggs: enrich the color and flavor, act as a rising agent. Use large eggs.
2. Butter: keep at room temperature before using. **3. Oil:** use a flavorless one like sunflower. **4. Confectioners' sugar:** used in icings. **5. Brown sugar:** good for rich cakes. **6. Demerara or dark brown sugar:** gives color and flavor to cakes. **7. Honey:** natural sugars such as honey can also be used. **8. Granulated or superfine sugar:** sweetens the cake mix, and whisked with eggs it adds volume and air into the cake. **9. Golden or raw sugar:** alternative to granulated sugar. **10. Self-rising flour:** this has a rising agent added and should only be used if specified. **11. All-purpose or cake flour:** forms the framework for the cake; use flours with a low gluten content for a soft, tender-crumb cake. **12. Rice flour:** alternative to cake flour. **13. Corn flour or cornstarch:** gluten-free flour.

CAKE SOS

1 **THE CAKE WAS TOO DRY** An insufficient amount of liquid or eggs was used. All cakes should be cooked with large free-range eggs; measure all wet liquids with a measuring cup.

TIP:
You leave most of the cakes in this book in the pan for about 10 minutes to cool and then turn them out onto a wire rack to cool completely.

2	**THE CAKE DIPPED IN THE MIDDLE** Sometimes caused by mix being spread unevenly in pan. Egg whites should be lightly folded in.	**3**	**THE CAKE CRACKED ON TOP** The cake can form a crust if oven is too hot or cake is placed too near direct heat. Place your cake on the middle shelf of the oven. However, this often happens to loaf cakes due to the shape of the pan.
4	**THE CAKE DID NOT RISE ENOUGH** Rising agent may have been left out, mix may have been over- or underbeaten or oven may have been too low. An oven thermometer is a great investment, as oven dials can be inaccurate. Cakes take longer to cook at a lower temperature, which dries them out.	**5**	**THE CAKE WAS UNEVEN, TOO BROWN OR BURNT** The oven is too hot and cake may have been left in the oven for too long. Buy an oven thermometer to check temperature.

CLASSIC BUTTERCREAM

❖ MAKES ENOUGH FOR 1 CAKE • PREPARATION: 10 MINUTES • BAKING: NONE ❖

½ cup (125 ml) unsalted butter, softened
2 cup (500 ml) confectioners' sugar
2 teaspoons (10 ml) boiling water,
   mixed with coffee extract or your choice
   of flavoring

FLAVOR AND COLOR VARIATIONS:
2 tablespoons (30 ml) cocoa powder
Finely grated zest of 1 lemon or orange

Several drops of natural food coloring mixed
   with 1 teaspoon (5 ml) boiling water

1 2
3 4

1	Using an electric mixer, cream the butter in a bowl until light and fluffy.	2	Sift in the confectioners' sugar and mix.
3	Add the coffee (as shown in photo), hot water, flavor or coloring of your choice and beat well, until combined.	4	Using a palette knife, spread the buttercream over your cake of choice.

CHOCOLATE GANACHE

❧ MAKES ENOUGH FOR 1 CAKE • PREPARATION: 10 MINUTES • BAKING: NONE ❧

5 ounces (150 g) dark chocolate (70% cocoa)
⅔ cup (150 ml) heavy cream (36%)

TIP:
If your ganache splits, either the chocolate has been overworked or heated too high. To remedy this, add a little milk to bring it together.

1 2
3 4

1	Break the chocolate into pieces and put into a heatproof bowl.	**2**	Pour the cream into a small pan and bring to a simmer until warm.
3	Pour the warm cream onto the chocolate and whisk to a thick, glossy sauce.	**4**	The ganache is now ready to use and can be spread over a cake or used as a filling.

CITRUS GLAZE

❧ MAKES ENOUGH FOR 1 CAKE • PREPARATION: 10 MINUTES • BAKING: NONE ❧

1⅓ cups + 1 tbsp (340 ml) confectioners' sugar
2 tablespoons (30 ml) unsalted butter, melted
4–6 tablespoons (60–90 ml) lemon, orange
  or lime juice
Natural food coloring

FLAVOR VARIATIONS:
1½ ounces (40 g) raspberries, strawberries,
  blueberries or a mixture
½ vanilla bean
3 tablespoons (45 ml) cocoa powder

Finely grated zest of 1 lemon, lime or orange
NOTE:
If flavoring with fresh fruit, do not use the
lemon, lime or orange juice.

1	Sift the confectioners' sugar into a bowl.	2	Add the melted butter to the sugar.
3	Add enough citrus juice, fresh fruit or other flavoring to make the consistency you desire. Add a food coloring if you wish to change the color.	4	Using a palette knife, spread the icing over your choice of cake.

MASCARPONE FROSTING

❧ MAKES ENOUGH FOR 1 CAKE • PREPARATION: 10 MINUTES • BAKING: NONE ❧

1¼ cups (300 ml) mascarpone cheese
4 tablespoons (60 ml) unsalted butter,
    melted and cooled
1½ cups (375 ml) confectioners' sugar
1 teaspoon (5 ml) vanilla extract

TIP:
Cut this recipe in half and use:
⅔ cup (150 ml) mascarpone cheese
2 tablespoons (30 ml) unsalted butter, melted
¾ cup (175 ml) confectioners' sugar
½ teaspoon (2 ml) vanilla extract

VARIATIONS:
Omit vanilla extract and add 3 tablespoons
(45 ml) cocoa powder
Add seeds from ½ vanilla bean

1	In a large bowl, beat the mascarpone cheese and butter with a handheld electric mixer until smooth.	2	Sift in the confectioners' sugar.
3	Add the vanilla extract and mix well.	4	Using a palette knife, spread thickly over your chosen cake.

SUGAR SYRUP

➤ MAKES ENOUGH FOR 1 CAKE • PREPARATION: 10 MINUTES • BAKING: NONE ➤

5 tablespoons (75 ml) granulated or
   superfine sugar
5 tablespoons (75 ml) liquid (water/alcohol/
   citrus juice)
Add any flavor you wish to use

FLAVOR VARIATIONS:
1 vanilla bean
Finely grated zest of 1 lemon or orange
Passion fruit pulp
Juice of 1 blood orange

TIPS:
If you would like to use this recipe for layer
cakes, double the quantities. Alcohol choices
include limoncello, crème de cassis, framboise,
brandy, etc.

1 2
3 4

1	Put the sugar and liquid, along with your preferred flavoring, into a small pan over low heat.	2	Allow the sugar to dissolve and the syrup to reduce until thick, about 4 to 5 minutes.
3	Take the pan off the heat and allow it to cool.	4	Once cool, remove the vanilla bean if using, and brush the syrup over your cake of choice.

CHOCOLATE CURLS

❧ MAKES ENOUGH FOR 1 CAKE • PREPARATION: 10 MINUTES • BAKING: NONE ❧

2¼ ounces (70 g) dark chocolate (70% cocoa) or white chocolate, broken into pieces

TIP:
These chocolate curls are very fragile and must be stored carefully in an airtight container. Use them within 1 to 2 days.

1	Put the chocolate in a heatproof bowl set over a pan of simmering water and leave until melted.	2	Spread the chocolate as thinly as possible over a non-stick surface (marble is preferable). Allow to cool and set for about 5 minutes.
3	Using a sharp knife or a palette knife and working away from you, scrape the chocolate to form curls.	4	Use to decorate your chosen cake.

MARSHMALLOW FLOWERS

➤ MAKES 10 FLOWERS • PREPARATION: 10 MINUTES • BAKING: NONE ◄

10 marshmallows
10 small store-bought sugar balls
Confectioners' sugar
Colored sugar or edible glitter, to dust

TIP:
Candies, such as chocolate-coated candies, jelly candies, etc., can be substituted for the sugar balls.

1 2
3 4

1	Hold a marshmallow on its "side" with the flat ends up and down.	2	Dip the blade tips of a pair of kitchen scissors into confectioners' sugar, then snip 5 evenly spaced cuts into the marshmallow, but don't cut all the way through.
3	Using a little confectioners' sugar, twist and fan out the marshmallows to form the "petals."	4	Overlap and press together the end petals (their sticky cut sides will hold them together), place a sugar ball at the center and dust with colored sugar or edible glitter.

MARBLED FRUITS

❧ MAKES ENOUGH FOR 1 CAKE • PREPARATION: 10 MINUTES + SETTING • BAKING: NONE ❧

2½ ounces (70 g) white chocolate, broken into pieces

3½ ounces (100 g) strawberries, cherries or physalis (cape gooseberry, ground cherry)

2½ ounces (70 g) dark chocolate, broken into pieces

TIP:
Don't overwork the chocolate by stirring it too much while it's melting.

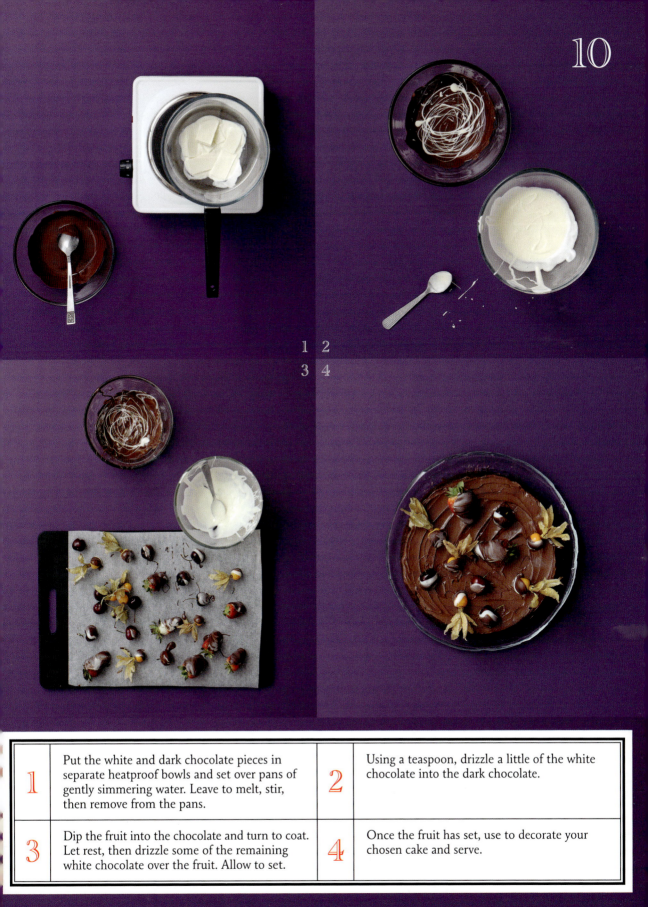

| 1 | 2 |
| 3 | 4 |

1	Put the white and dark chocolate pieces in separate heatproof bowls and set over pans of gently simmering water. Leave to melt, stir, then remove from the pans.	2	Using a teaspoon, drizzle a little of the white chocolate into the dark chocolate.
3	Dip the fruit into the chocolate and turn to coat. Let rest, then drizzle some of the remaining white chocolate over the fruit. Allow to set.	4	Once the fruit has set, use to decorate your chosen cake and serve.

SIMPLE CAKES

2

LIGHT CAKES

DENSER CAKES

CAKES WITH FRUIT

BUTTER CAKE

❖ SERVES 8 TO 10 • PREPARATION: 15 MINUTES • BAKING TIME: 35 TO 40 MINUTES ❖

⅞ cup (225 ml) unsalted butter, softened
1½ cups (375 ml) granulated or superfine
   sugar
3 eggs
3 egg yolks
3 cups (750 ml) cake flour

2½ teaspoons (12 ml) baking powder
¼ teaspoon (1 ml) salt
1¼ cups (300 ml) milk
¾ cup (175 ml) flaked almonds
Finely grated zest of 1 lemon

DECORATION:
Citrus glaze (see recipe 5)
IN ADVANCE:
Grease a 9-inch (23 cm) Bundt pan.
Preheat oven to 350°F (160°C).

1 2
3 4

1	Beat the butter and sugar for about 4 to 5 minutes, until light and fluffy.	2	Add the eggs and egg yolks and beat to combine.	
3	Sift the flour and baking powder into a bowl and add the salt.	4	Add the flour mixture to the stand mixer, then stir in the milk and beat for 3 minutes.	➤

5 6
7 8

5	Add the flaked almonds and grated lemon zest, or a flavor of your choice, and mix well.	6	Scrape the batter into the prepared pan and bake in the preheated oven for 35 to 40 minutes.
7	Leave the cake in the mold for about 10 minutes, then turn out onto a wire rack to cool completely.	8	Spread the citrus glaze over the cake.

9

Allow the icing to set before eating.

FLAVOR VARIATIONS
❋

If you would like to add other flavorings to the cake mix, try:
5 ounces (150 g), about 1 cup (250 ml), of fresh raspberries, lightly mashed.
⅓ to ½ cup (75 to 125 ml) of toffee or caramel sauce with finely grated orange zest.
¾ cup (175 ml) of flaked almonds and finely grated lemon zest.

GLUTEN-FREE CAKE

❧ SERVES 6 TO 8 • PREPARATION: 15 MINUTES • BAKING TIME: 25 TO 30 MINUTES ❧

⅓ cup (75 ml) rice flour
3 tablespoons (45 ml) corn flour
2 teaspoons (10 ml) baking powder
¼ cup (60 ml) ground almonds
½ cup (125 ml) butter, softened
⅔ cup (150 ml) granulated or superfine sugar

3 eggs
1 vanilla bean, seeds scraped out
DECORATION: Lemon syrup (see recipe 7)
½ cup (125 ml) mascarpone cheese
1 tablespoon (15 ml) confectioners' sugar,

plus extra to dust
6½ ounces (180 g) strawberries, cut into quarters
IN ADVANCE: Grease, flour (with rice flour) and line an 8-inch (20 cm) round cake pan. Preheat oven to 350°F (180°C).

1	Sift the flours and baking powder into a bowl and add the ground almonds.	2	Add butter, sugar, eggs and vanilla and whisk until mixed. Pour into prepared pan.	3	Bake for 25 to 30 minutes. Cool in pan for 10 minutes, then turn out onto rack.
4	While cake is cooling, whisk the mascarpone and confectioners' sugar together.	5	Put the cooled cake on a plate and brush with the lemon syrup.	6	Spread the mascarpone over and add strawberries. Dust with confectioners' sugar. **NOTE:** the mixture maybe slightly runnier than a normal cake mixture

ANGEL FOOD CAKE

❧ SERVES 14 TO 16 • PREPARATION: 15 MINUTES • BAKING TIME: 40 TO 45 MINUTES ❧

1¼ cups (300 ml) cake flour
1½ cups (375 ml) granulated or
   superfine sugar
12 egg whites
1 teaspoon (5 ml) vanilla extract

1 teaspoon (5 ml) cream of tartar
Pinch of salt
Lemon syrup (see recipe 7)
Citrus glaze icing (see recipe 5)
7 ounces (200 g) fresh summer berries

IN ADVANCE:
Preheat oven to 350°F (180°C). Make sure
a 10-inch (25 cm) tube pan is clean and
dry. Any amount of oil or residue could
deflate the egg whites.

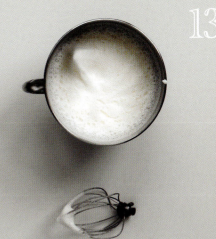

1	Sift the flour and ½ cup (125 ml) of the sugar together and set aside.	2	Whisk the egg whites, vanilla, cream of tartar and salt together to form medium-stiff peaks.
3	While whisking, gradually add the remaining sugar to form stiff peaks.	4	Using a metal spoon, gradually fold the sifted flour mixture into the egg whites, one-third at a time. Do not overmix. ➢

5 6

5	Put the cake batter into the tube pan. Bake for 40 to 45 minutes, until the cake springs back when touched.	6	Allow to cool, balancing the tube pan upside down on a wire rack to prevent decompression.
7	When cooked, run a knife around the edge of the pan and invert the cake onto a plate.	8	Brush the top of the cake with the syrup.

 Spread the icing over the cake and decorate with summer fruits.

TIP
❋

For a light chocolate cake, replace ⅓ cup (75 ml) of flour with ⅓ cup (75 ml) of cocoa powder.

CLASSIC FRUIT CAKE

❧ SERVES 8 TO 10 • PREPARATION: 15 MINUTES • BAKING TIME: 1½ TO 2 HOURS ☙

¾ cup (175 ml) unsalted butter, softened
¾ cup (175 ml) raw or turbinado sugar
Finely grated zest of 1 orange
4 eggs
1⅓ cups (325 ml) all-purpose or cake flour
Small pinch of salt
½ teaspoon (2 ml) pumpkin pie spices

1 teaspoon (5 ml) baking powder
⅔ cup (150 ml) ground almonds
2 tablespoons (30 ml) corn syrup
4 ounces (120 g) each currants, raisins and
  sultanas
2 ounces (60 g) mixed peel
2 tablespoons (30 ml) good-quality brandy

DECORATION:
⅓ cup (175 ml) whole blanched almonds
IN ADVANCE:
Grease and line an 8-inch (20 cm) round
cake pan. Preheat oven to 300°F (150°C).

1	Beat the butter, sugar and orange zest together until light and fluffy.	2	Add the eggs and mix well.	3	Sift in flour, salt, spices and baking powder. Add ground almonds and syrup; mix.
4	Add the dried fruit and brandy and mix well.	5	Spoon into prepared pan and bake for 1½ to 2 hours. Halfway through baking, arrange the whole almonds on top.	6	Allow the cake to cool in the pan before serving. This cake will keep well for a couple of weeks if stored in an airtight container.

SIMNEL CAKE

❧ SERVES 8-10 • PREPARATION: 20 MINUTES • BAKING TIME: 2 HOURS ❧

Fruit cake mixture to step 4 (see recipe 14)
1 pound (500 g) marzipan
5 tablespoons (75 ml) apricot jam

IN ADVANCE:
Grease and line an 8-inch (20 cm) round cake pan and preheat oven to 300°F (150°C).

TIP:
You can decorate the top of the cake with some edible flowers if you like.

1	Spoon half of the cake mix into the prepared pan, making sure it is level.	2	Roll one-third of the marzipan out to the size of the pan and put on top of the cake.	3	Spoon remaining mix on top and level surface. Bake for 2 hours. Cool in pan.
4	Heat the apricot jam in a small pan and brush the cake with the jam.	5	Set 2 ounces (50 g) aside, roll out remaining marzipan and put on cake. Make 12 balls with rest of marzipan.	6	Pinch sides of marzipan. Decorate with the balls, using jam to secure. Finish with edible flowers, if desired.

CARROT & WALNUT CAKE

❧ SERVES 10 TO 12 • PREPARATION: 30 MINUTES • BAKING TIME: 40 MINUTES ❧

⅞ cup (225 ml) unsalted butter, softened
1¾ cups (375 ml) granulated or superfine sugar
4 eggs
1⅓ cups (325 ml) self-rising flour
1½ teaspoons (7 ml) baking powder
Pinch each of allpice, cinnamon and salt

Finely grated zest of 1 lemon
1¾ cups (425 ml) walnuts, roughly chopped
12½ ounces (350 g) carrots, grated
TOPPING:
⅓ cups + 2 tablespoons (100 ml) mascarpone
⅓ cups+ 2 tablespoons (100 ml) cream cheese

7 tablespoons (100 ml) confectioners' sugar
Juice and finely grated zest of 1 lemon
⅔ cup (150 ml) walnuts
IN ADVANCE:
Grease and line a 9-inch (23 cm) springform
pan. Preheat oven to 350°F (180°C).

1 2
3 4

1	Beat the butter and sugar together until light and fluffy.	2	Beat in the eggs.
3	Sift in the flour, baking powder, spices and salt and mix to combine.	4	Add the lemon zest, walnuts and carrots and beat well. ➤

5	Spoon the mixture into the prepared pan and bake for about 40 minutes, until well risen and firm to the touch.	6	Allow the cake to cool in the pan for 10 minutes before turning out onto a wire rack to cool completely.
7	For the topping, put the mascarpone, cream cheese, confectioners' sugar, lemon zest and juice in a bowl and whisk for 1 minute.	8	Using a palette knife, spread the topping thickly over the top of the cake.

| 9 | Lightly smash the walnuts on a chopping board with a rolling pin and arrange them on top of the cake to decorate. | **VARIATIONS**
❋
For a change, use different nuts, such as pecans, or use the finely grated zest and juice of 2 oranges instead of the lemons. |

APPLE CAKE WITH CRUMB TOPPING

✤ SERVES 8 TO 10 • PREPARATION: 20 MINUTES • BAKING TIME: 60 MINUTES ✤

⅔ cup (150 ml) unsalted butter, softened
¼ cup (60 ml) packed brown sugar
3 eggs
⅓ cup + 2 tbsp (100 ml) good-quality honey
Finely grated zest and juice of 1 orange
3 tablespoons (45 ml) milk

2 cups (500 ml) cake flour
1 teaspoon (5 ml) baking soda
1 teaspoon (5 ml) baking powder
¼ teaspoon (1 ml) ground cinnamon
½ cup (125 ml) quick-cooking rolled oats
⅓ cup (75 ml) chopped walnuts

10 ounces (300 g) tart apples, thinly sliced
TOPPING:
1⅓ cups (325 ml) fruit and nut granola
IN ADVANCE: Line an 8-inch (20 cm)
round cake pan with parchment paper.
Preheat oven to 350°F (180°C).

1	Cream the butter and brown sugar together until light and fluffy.	2	Beat in the eggs, honey, finely grated orange zest, juice and milk.	
3	Sift the flour, baking soda, baking powder and cinnamon into another bowl and add the oats.	4	Add the flour to the creamed mixture and stir in the walnuts. Set aside.	➤

5 Spoon half of the cake mixture into the prepared pan. Arrange the apples on top, then add the remaining cake mixture. Top with the granola.

NOTE
❊

This cake is best served warm with hot custard.

	Bake for 20 minutes, then lower the temperature to 325°F (160°C) and bake for a further 40 minutes. Allow the cake to cool slightly before serving.	**VARIATION** ❈
6		For a slightly nuttier topping, replace the granola with the same amount of chopped mixed nuts.

PINEAPPLE POUND CAKE

❧ SERVES 14 TO 16 • PREPARATION: 20 MINUTES • BAKING TIME: 50 TO 60 MINUTES ❧

2 cups (500 ml) unsalted butter, softened
2½ cups (625 ml) granulated or
   superfine sugar
8 eggs
4 cups (1 L) self-rising flour
2 teaspoons (10 ml) baking powder

Good pinch of salt
⅓ cup + 1 tablespoon (90 ml) chopped
   canned pineapple
Finely grated zest of 1 orange
2 vanilla beans, seeds scraped out
4 canned pineapple rings, cut in half

GLAZE: 4 tablespoons (60 ml) store-
bought apricot glaze
IN ADVANCE:
Grease and flour a 9½-inch (24 cm) Bundt
pan. Preheat oven to 300°F (150°C).

1 2
3 4

1	Beat the butter, sugar, eggs, flour, baking powder, salt chopped pineapple, orange zest and vanilla together until combined.	2	Place the halved pineapple rings into the base of the Bundt pan.	
3	Pour the cake mixture on top and bake for 50 to 60 minutes.	4	Allow the cake to cool in the pan for 30 minutes, then turn out onto a wire rack.	➤

| 5 | Brush the apricot glaze over the cake. | **TIP**
❈
You can use smooth apricot jam instead of the apricot glaze if you prefer. |

6	Serve the cake warm or at room temperature with hot custard or toffee or caramel sauce.	**DIFFERENT FLAVORS** ❋ Orange Pound Cake: Add finely grated orange zest and seeds from 2 vanilla beans; put 5 orange slices in the base of the mold. Apple Pound Cake: Add finely grated lemon zest and seeds from 2 vanilla beans; put ½ cup (125 ml) of chopped apple into the cake mix and 2 sliced apples in the base of the mold.

GENOISE (SPONGE CAKE)

❧ SERVES 8 TO 10 • PREPARATION: 20 MINUTES • BAKING TIME: 25 TO 30 MINUTES ❧

2 tablespoons (30 ml) unsalted butter
3 eggs
7 tablespoons (100 ml) granulated or
   superfine sugar
⅔ cup (150 ml) cake flour
Small pinch of salt

DECORATION:
3½ ounces (100 g) summer fruits
⅔ cup (150 ml) heavy cream (36%), whipped
A little icing sugar, to dust

IN ADVANCE:
Grease and line an 8-inch (20 cm) spring-form pan. Preheat oven to 350ºF (180ºC).
TIP: This is a great basic recipe to use with other fillings or as a trifle base.

1	Melt the butter in a pan over a low heat, then allow to cool.	2	Whisk the eggs and sugar for about 6 to 8 minutes, until very light and pale.	3	Lightly fold in the flour, salt and butter.
4	Spoon the mix into the prepared pan and bake for 25 to 30 minutes, until risen and golden.	5	Remove the cake from the pan and allow to cool on a wire rack.	6	Serve with summer tfruits and whipped cream and a dusting of confectioners' sugar.

YOGURT CAKE

➤ SERVES 8 TO 10 • PREPARATION: 15 MINUTES • BAKING TIME: 45 TO 50 MINUTES ➤

1½ cups (375 ml) granulated or
    superfine sugar
⅓ cup (75 ml) unsalted butter, softened
Small pinch of salt
3 eggs, separated
1 cup (250 ml) Greek yogurt

Finely grated zest of 1 lemon
1⅔ cups (400 ml) self-rising flour
GARNISH:
Citrus glaze (see recipe 5)
Thinly sliced lemons

IN ADVANCE:
Grease and line a 9-inch (23 cm) round
cake pan with removable bottom. Preheat
oven to 350°F (180°C).

1	Whisk the sugar, butter, salt and egg yolks together until well combined and smooth.	2	Add the yogurt and lemon zest and whisk well.	3	Sift in the flour and whisk to combine.
4	In a clean bowl, whisk the egg whites until soft peaks form.	5	Carefully fold the egg whites into the yogurt mixture.	6	Spoon the mix into the prepared pan and bake for 45 to 50 minutes.

7

Allow the cake to cool in the pan for 10 minutes, then turn out onto a wire rack and allow it to cool completely.

TIP

The cooked cake should be well risen and firm when you touch it with a fingertip.

8	Spread the citrus glaze over the top of the cooled cake and garnish with lemon slices.

DIFFERENT FLAVORS
❋

Omit the lemon zest for different flavor variations.
Pineapple Yogurt Cake: Add ½ cup (125 ml) of finely chopped fresh pineapple; decorate with icing and pineapple slices.
Apple Yogurt Cake: Add ½ cup (125 ml) of peeled and chopped apples; decorate with icing and apple slices.

BROWN SUGAR BANANA CAKE

❖ SERVES 10 TO 12 • PREPARATION: 20 MINUTES • BAKING TIME: 35 TO 40 MINUTES ❖

6 ripe bananas
3 eggs
⅔ cup (150 ml) packed brown sugar
¼ cup (60 ml) vegetable oil
½ teaspoon (2 ml) ground cinnamon
1 cup (250 ml) mixed nuts, chopped

1⅓ cups (325 ml) self-rising flour
Small pinch of salt
TOPPING:
½ cup (125 ml) mixed nuts, chopped
½ teaspoon (2 ml) ground cinnamon

IN ADVANCE:
Grease and line a 9-inch (23 cm) round cake pan. Preheat oven to 350°F (180°C).

1	Peel the bananas, put in a bowl and mash with a potato masher to make a rough purée. Set aside.	2	Put the eggs and sugar in another bowl and whisk for about 5 to 10 minutes, until light.
3	Add the oil and cinnamon to the egg mixture and mix to combine.	4	Add the nuts, flour, salt and bananas and mix until well combined, then pour into the prepared pan. ➢

| 5 | Sprinkle the nuts and cinnamon on top of the cake and bake for 35 to 40 minutes, until golden and a skewer inserted into the center of the cake comes out clean. | **TIP** ❋
Chop the bananas roughly before mashing to help them break down into a purée. Make sure you use ripe bananas. |

6   Allow the cake to cool in the pan for 5 mintes, then serve warm with crème fraîche, if desired.

NOTE
*

This cake is also great served with Greek-style yogurt or scoops of good-quality ice cream.

PLUM & ALMOND CAKE

❖ SERVES 8 TO 10 • PREPARATION: 20 MINUTES • BAKING TIME: 35 TO 40 MINUTES ❖

⅞ cup (200 ml) unsalted butter, softened
⅞ cup (200 ml), superfine sugar
1 vanilla bean
1¾ cups (425 ml) ground almonds
7 tablespoons (100 ml) Manuka honey
⅓ cup + 1 tablespoon (90 ml) self-rising flour

Small pinch of salt
4 eggs
4 plums
GLAZE:
4 teaspoons (20 ml) unsalted butter
4 tablespoons (60 ml) Manuka honey

IN ADVANCE:
Grease and line a 9-inch (23 cm) round
cake pan. Preheat oven to 350ºF (180ºC).

1	Beat the butter and sugar together for about 2 to 3 minutes, until light and fluffy.	2	Cut the vanilla bean in half, scrape out the seeds and mix in.	
3	Add the almonds, honey, flour, salt and eggs and beat for 1 minute.	4	Halve and pit the plums, then cut into quarters.	➤

5   Spoon the mixture into the prepared pan and arrange the plums on top. Bake for 35 to 40 minutes, until well risen and golden.

NOTE
❋

You can use a couple of drops of good-quality vanilla extract instead of the vanilla bean, if you like.

6 Put the butter and honey in a small pan and heat until the butter has melted, then brush the glaze over the cake.

TIP
❋

Use some of your best honey, as the flavor really comes through. I often use Greek honey from Kefallonia instead of Manuka (which is from New Zealand).

PEACH UPSIDE-DOWN CAKE

❧ SERVES 6 TO 8 • PREPARATION: 15 MINUTES • BAKING TIME: 35 TO 40 MINUTES ❧

1¼ pounds (600 g) fresh peaches
¼ (60 ml) unsalted butter, softened
⅔ cup (150 ml) packed light brown sugar
1⅔ cups (400 ml) self-rising flour
½ cup (125 ml) ground almonds

½ teaspoon (2 ml) salt
Finely grated zest of 1 orange
⅓ cup (75 ml) mixed dried fruit
1 cup (250 ml) whole milk
2 eggs

GARNISH:
½ cup (125 ml) pecans
IN ADVANCE:
You will need a 10-inch (25 cm) ovenproof
frying pan. Preheat oven to 350°F (180°C).

1

4

2

5

3

6

1	Halve and pit the peaches and cut into quarters.	2	Melt the butter in the frying pan. Add half the brown sugar and cook for 5 minutes.	3	Add the peach quarters to the pan and cook for 3 to 4 minutes.
4	Take off the heat and spread the peaches out, upside down, in a single layer.	5	Sift the flour and almonds; add the salt, orange zest, dried fruit and mix.	6	Add the milk, eggs and the rest of the brown sugar and mix. ➤

1 2
3 4

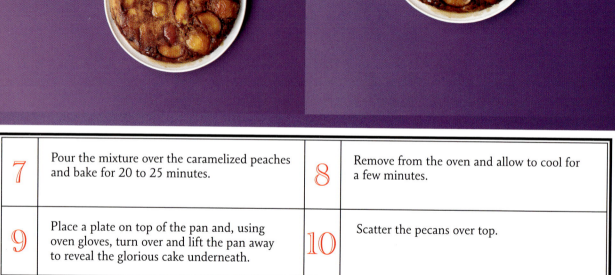

7	Pour the mixture over the caramelized peaches and bake for 20 to 25 minutes.	8	Remove from the oven and allow to cool for a few minutes.
9	Place a plate on top of the pan and, using oven gloves, turn over and lift the pan away to reveal the glorious cake underneath.	10	Scatter the pecans over top.

This cake is best served warm with good-quality ice cream.

VARIATION
❋

If peaches are out of season, or for a change, use plums or fresh apricots instead.

BLOOD ORANGE & ALMOND CAKE

❧ SERVES 8 TO 10 • PREPARATION: 20 MINUTES • BAKING TIME: 60 TO 65 MINUTES ❧

1¼ cups (300 ml) unsalted butter, softened
1½ cups (375 ml) granulated or superfine
   sugar
3½ cups (875 ml) finely ground almonds
2 teaspoons (10 ml) vanilla extract
5 eggs

Finely grated zest and juice of 1 blood orange
1 cup (250 ml) stone ground cornmeal
1 teaspoon (5 ml) baking powder
Good pinch of salt
TOPPING:
2 whole blood oranges

⅓ cup (75 ml) whole almonds
Blood orange syrup (see recipe 7)
IN ADVANCE:
Grease a deep 9-inch (23 cm) round cake
pan. Preheat oven to 325ºF (170ºC).

1

2

3

4

5

6

1	Beat the butter and sugar together until light and fluffy.	2	Stir in the ground almonds and vanilla, then add the eggs.	3	Add the blood orange zest and juice, cornmeal, baking powder and salt.	
4	Slice the blood oranges and arrange in the base of the prepared pan.	5	Spoon the mixture into the pan and bake for 60 to 65 minutes, until golden.	6	Leave for 10 minutes, then turn out and let cool slightly.	➤

		TIP
7	While the cake is still warm, brush the blood orange syrup the top.	❋
		Once the cake is cooked, leave it to rest in the pan for 10 minutes, then turn it out and allow it to cool upside down for about 5 minutes.

8 Smash the almonds and sprinkle over the cake; serve warm.

VARIATION
❊

You can also do this recipe with slices of pineapple instead of blood oranges, if you prefer.

LAYER CAKES

OLD FAVORITES

CAKES WITH NUTS

LIGHT CREAM CAKES

BATTENBERG CAKE

❖ SERVES 4 TO 6 • PREPARATION: 40 MINUTES • BAKING TIME: 25 TO 30 MINUTES ❖

7 tablespoons (100 ml) unsalted butter
½ cup (125 ml) granulated or superfine sugar
2 eggs
¾ cup (175 ml) self-rising flour
½ cup (125 ml) ground almonds

1 teaspoon (5 ml) red food coloring
Confectioners' sugar, for rolling out
SIDES:
8 ounces (250 g) good-quality marzipan
2½ tablespoons (37 ml) apricot jam

IN ADVANCE:
Grease an 8-inch (20 cm) square cake pan. Put a piece of foil in pan to form a barrier between the two cake mixtures. Preheat oven to 325ºF (160ºC).

1	Cream the butter and sugar together until light and fluffy.	2	Add the eggs, sift in the flour and ground almonds and mix.	3	Divide the batter into 2 equal parts. Add food coloring to one part.
4	Put pink mix into one side of prepared pan and plain mix in other. Bake for 25 to 30 minutes.	5	Leave the cake to stand for 5 minutes.	6	Cool cake on a wire rack. Remove foil and separate cakes.

7	Trim the edges of both cakes and cut each cake lengthwise into 2 strips about 1½ inches (4 cm) wide.	8	Lightly heat the apricot jam in a pan.
9	Brush the jam on the sides of the cake pieces to glue 2 pink and 2 white strips together in checkerboard fashion. Spread all 4 sides of the completed cake with jam.	10	Roll out the marzipan about ⅛ inch (3 mm) thick on a surface lightly dusted with confectioners' sugar. Cut to fit the length of cake and cover all sides, leaving the ends open.

11	Lay the cake on one end of the marzipan and wrap to completely enclose all 4 sides of the cake, pinching the marzipan to seal. Place the cake, sealed side down, on a serving plate and slice.	Use a little less food coloring for a lighter color, and substitute apricot jam for seedless raspberry jam.

COFFEE-FLAVORED CAKE

❧ SERVES 12 TO 14 • PREPARATION: 20 MINUTES • BAKING TIME: 35 TO 40 MINUTES ❧

1½ cups (375 ml) hazelnuts
4 eggs
1 cup + 2 tablespoons (275 ml) packed
   brown sugar
3 tablespoons (45 ml) coffee extract

¾ cup + 3 tablespoons (220 ml) butter
   softened
1¾ cups (425 ml) self-rising flour
1 teaspoon (5 ml) baking powder
TOPPING:
Coffee buttercream (see recipe 3)

GARNISH:
½ cup (125 ml) chocolate-covered
   coffee beans
IN ADVANCE:
Grease and line two 8-inch (20 cm) round
cake pans. Preheat oven to 350°F (180°C).

1	Toast the nuts on a baking sheet in the oven for 5 minutes, until golden. Allow to cool.	2	Chop the cooled hazelnuts and reserve ½ cup (125 ml) for the top.	3	Beat the eggs, brown sugar and coffee extract for 3 minutes, until well blended.
4	Add the butter, flour, baking powder and chopped nuts and mix for 3 minutes.	5	Spoon the mix into the prepared pans. Bake for 35 to 40 minutes, until well risen.	6	Cool in pans for 10 minutes; turn out on a rack and let cool. ➤

		VARIATION
7	Put one of the cakes onto a serving plate and spread on some of the buttercream, then put the other cake on top.	Instead of hazelnuts, use walnuts or pecans.

8	Spread the remaining buttercream over and along the sides of the cake. Top with the remaining chopped hazelnuts and chocolate-covered coffee beans.	**DIFFERENT FLAVORS** ❊
		Cooled espresso can replace the coffee extract, for a stronger coffee flavor.

VICTORIA SPONGE CAKE

❧ SERVES 6 TO 8 • PREPARATION: 15 MINUTES • BAKING TIME: 15 TO 20 MINUTES ❧

¾ cup (175 ml) unsalted butter, softened
1 cup (250 ml) granulated or superfine sugar
1⅔ cups (400 ml) self-rising flour
2 teaspoons (10 ml) baking powder
4 eggs
Finely grated zest of 1 lemon

FILLING:
¾ cup (175 ml) double cream (48%) or
   crème fraîche
8 ounces (250 g) fresh raspberries
Juice of ½ lemon

GARNISH:
3 tablespoons (45 ml) granulated or
   superfine sugar
IN ADVANCE:
Grease and line two 9-inch (23 cm) round
baking pans. Preheat oven to 350°F (180°C).

1	Beat all the cake ingredients together until thoroughly blended.	2	Divide the mixture evenly between the prepared pans and bake for 20 minutes. Allow to cool on a wire rack.
3	For the filling, whip the cream in a bowl until it forms soft peaks.	4	Put the raspberries in a bowl and add the lemon juice. Mash lightly, leaving some whole for texture.

| 5 | When the cakes are completely cooled, spread the cream and then the raspberry mixture over one cake. Sandwich the cakes together. | **TIP**
❊
Make sure the cakes are cooked. To test, insert a skewer in the middle. If it comes out clean, then the cakes are done. If not, put back in the oven for a bit longer. |

	Sprinkle sugar over the top and serve.	**VARIATIONS** ❁
6		In summertime, make the most of the strawberry season and use these instead of raspberries. Use your favorite jam instead of the fresh raspberries for the middle of the cake.

BISCUIT DE SAVOIE

❧ SERVES 6 • PREPARATION: 20 MINUTES • BAKING TIME: 20 TO 25 MINUTES ❧

4 eggs, separated
⅔ cup (150 ml) granulated or superfine sugar
½ cup (125 ml) cake flour
Good pinch of salt

FILLING:
⅔ cup (150 ml) heavy cream (36%), whipped
3 tablespoons (45 ml) sweetened chestnut
  puree

GARNISH:
Dark chocolate curls (see recipe 8)
A little confectioners' sugar, to dust
IN ADVANCE:
Grease and flour an 8-inch (20 cm) round
cake pan. Preheat oven to 350°F (180°C).

1	Whisk the egg yolks and sugar together until light, about 4 to 5 minutes.	2	Sift in the flour and mix well.	3	Beat the egg whites with salt in a clean bowl until they form stiff peaks.
4	Fold the egg whites into the egg yolk mixture, lifting the batter to incorporate air.	5	Pour the mixture into the prepared pan. Bake for 20 minutes. Cool in the pan.	6	Cut the cake in half and put one half on a serving plate.

| 7 | In a large bowl, mix the whipped cream and chestnut puree. | **VARIATION**
❀
Mix the whipped cream with lemon curd and replace the dark chocolate curls with white chocloate curls. |

| 8 | Spread the chestnut cream over the cake base and sandwich the two halves together. Dust with confectioners' sugar, place dark chocolate curls on top and serve. | **VARIATION**
✳
Use chocolate ganache (see recipe 4) for a chocolate biscuit. Fill the cake with the ganache, dust with cocoa powder and decorate with chocolate curls. |

LEMON & POPPY SEED CAKE

❖ SERVES 8 TO 10 • PREPARATION: 20 MINUTES • BAKING TIME: 30 TO 35 MINUTES ❖

1⅓ cups (325 ml) granulated or
   superfine sugar
3 eggs
2 cups (500 ml) self-rising flour
⅞ cup (200 ml) butter, melted
Finely grated zest of 2 lemons

Juice of 1 lemon
1 tablespoon (15 ml) poppy seeds
FILLING:
¾ cup (175 ml) mascarpone cheese
2 tablespoons (30 ml) limoncello liqueur

GARNISH:
Citrus glaze (see recipe 5), zest of 1 lemon
½ lemon
1 teaspoon (5 ml) poppy seeds
IN ADVANCE:
Grease and line a 9-inch (23 cm) round
cake pan. Preheat oven to 350ºF (180ºC).

1	Whisk the sugar and eggs together until light and fluffy.	2	Add the flour and melted butter, lemon zest, juice and poppy seeds. Mix again for 1 minute, until well combined.	
3	Spoon the mixture into the prepared pan and bake for 30 to 35 minutes, until golden. Leave to cool on a wire rack, then cut the cake in half.	4	In a bowl, mix together the mascarpone and limoncello. Spread thickly over one of the halves of the cakes.	➤

	Place the domed half of the cake on top of the filling and spread the citrus glaze over the cake.	**TIP**
5		The cake is cooked when a skewer inserted into the middle comes out clean.

6 Thinly slice the ½ lemon and arrange decoratively on top of the cake. Finally, sprinkle with poppy seeds.

VARIATION
✻

Try substituting the lemons with clementines for a great Christmastime treat!

WALNUT LAYER CAKE

❧ SERVES 12 TO 14 • PREPARATION: 20 MINUTES • BAKING TIME: 15 TO 20 MINUTES ❧

¾ cup + 3 tablespoons (220 ml) unsalted
    butter, melted
1 cup + 2 tablespoons (280 ml) packed
    muscovado or light brown sugar
3 eggs

1⅓ cups (325 ml) self-rising flour
2 teaspoons (10 ml) baking powder
2 cups (500 ml) walnuts, chopped

GARNISH:
Coffee buttercream (see recipe 3)
⅔ cup (150 ml) crushed walnuts
IN ADVANCE:
Line three 9-inch (23 cm) round cake pans.
Preheat oven to 350°F (180°C).

1	Mix all the cake ingredients together.	2	Spoon the mix into the prepared pans. Bake for 15 to 20 minutes. Cool in pans for 10 minutes.	3	Turn the cakes out onto a wire rack and allow to cool.
4	Spread buttercream over one cake, put a cake on top, add buttercream and third cake.	5	Spread the remaining buttercream over the top and sides of the cake.	6	Decorate with walnut pieces on the top and around the sides.

MANGO & PISTACHIO CAKE

SERVES 10 TO 12 • PREPARATION: 40 MINUTES • BAKING TIME: 25 TO 30 MINUTES

¾ cups + 3 tablespoons (220 ml) unsalted butter, softened
1 cup + 2 tablespoons (280 ml) granulated or superfine sugar
4 eggs
1 cup (250 ml) pistachio nuts
1¾ cups (425 ml) self-rising flour
2 teaspoons (10 ml) baking powder
2¼ ounces (70 g) dried mango, finely chopped
2 tablespoons (30 ml) rose water

FROSTING: 2 egg whites
1¾ cups (425 ml) granulated or superfine sugar
4 tablespoons (60 ml) rose water
½ teaspoon (5 ml) cream of tartar
1 ripe mango, peeled and sliced

IN ADVANCE: Grease and line three 9-inch (23 cm) round cake pans. Preheat oven to 325°F (160°C).

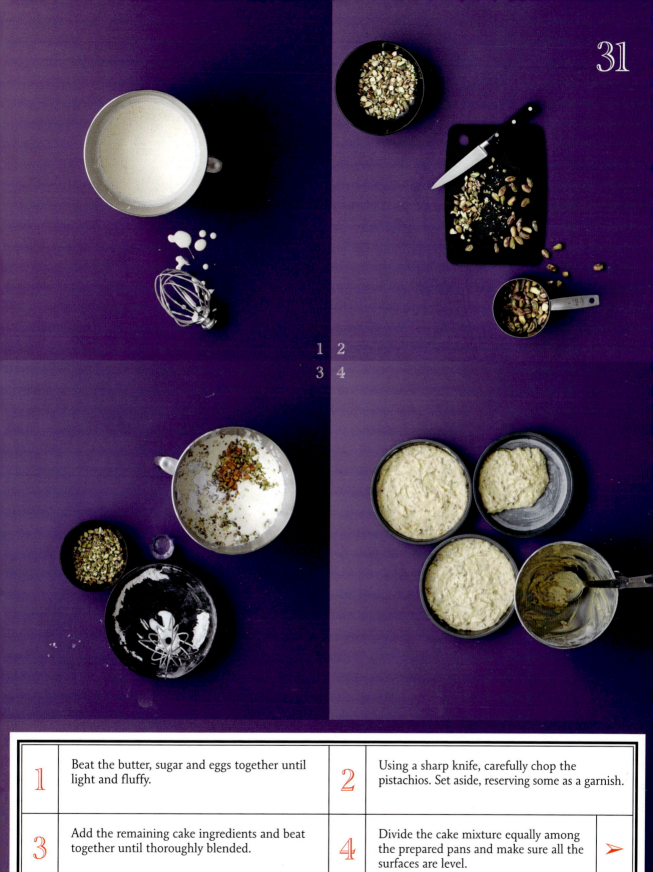

1	Beat the butter, sugar and eggs together until light and fluffy.	2	Using a sharp knife, carefully chop the pistachios. Set aside, reserving some as a garnish.
3	Add the remaining cake ingredients and beat together until thoroughly blended.	4	Divide the cake mixture equally among the prepared pans and make sure all the surfaces are level. ➤

5	Bake for 25 to 30 minutes, until golden and springy to the touch. Turn out of the pans and allow to cool on wire racks.	6	Put the egg whites, sugar, rose water and cream of tartar in a heatproof bowl over a pan of simmering water and whisk until thick.
7	Sandwich the cake layers together with a little of the frosting.	8	Use the remaining frosting to cover the top and sides of the cake.

9 Decorate with sliced mango and sprinkle over the reserved chopped pistachios, if desired.

VARIATION
❖

For a sweeter flavor, use Alphonso mangos when available.

SALTED CARAMEL CAKE

✦ SERVES 10 TO 12 • PREPARATION: 20 MINUTES • BAKING TIME: 15 TO 20 MINUTES, PLUS CHILLING TIME ✦

¾ cup + 3 tablespoons (220 ml) unsalted butter, softened

1 cup + 2 tablespoons (225 ml) packed muscovado or light brown sugar

3 eggs

1⅓ cups (325 ml) self-rising flour

2 teaspoons (10 ml) baking powder

2 cups (500 ml) blanched almonds, chopped

FILLING:

4 teaspoons (20 ml) unsalted butter, softened

½ cup (125 ml) packed dark brown sugar

1 can condensed milk (14 ounces/398 ml)

Large pinch of sea salt

2 to 3 tablespoons (30 to 45 ml) water

GARNISH:

3 tablespoons (45 ml) toasted sliced almonds

Pinch of sea salt

IN ADVANCE: Grease and line three 8-inch (20 cm) round cake pans. Preheat oven to 350ºF (180ºC).

1 2
3 4

1	Mix all the cake ingredients together until smooth.	2	Spoon the mixture into the prepared pans. Bake for 15 to 20 minutes, until firm to the touch. Allow to cool in the pans for 10 minutes.
3	Turn out of the pans and allow to cool on wire racks.	4	Gently melt the butter and sugar over low heat until the sugar dissolves and turns a deep brown. ➤

5 | 6
7 | 8

5	Add the condensed milk and salt and stir for 2 to 3 minutes. Cool slightly. Add 2 to 3 tablespoons (30 to 40 ml) water to make it more spreadable.	6	Put one of the cakes on a serving plate and top with some of the caramel mixture.
7	Layer the cakes with the caramel mix between each cake.	8	Spread the remaining caramel mix on top of the last cake and chill for about 30 to 40 minutes, until firm.

9 | When firm, sprinkle the cake with flaked almonds and a little more salt.

VARIATIONS
❋

For a creamier finish, substitute the caramel sauce with 1¼ cups (300 ml) heavy cream (36%), whipped, between the layers. You can also replace the almonds with the same amount of Brazil nuts.

RED VELVET CAKE

❧ **SERVES 10 TO 12 • PREPARATION: 40 MINUTES • BAKING TIME: 25 TO 30 MINUTES** ❧

2½ cups (625 ml) self-rising flour
1 teaspoon (5 ml) salt
2 tablespoons (30 ml) cocoa powder
1⅓ cups (275 ml) sugar
¾ cup (175 ml) vegetable oil

2 eggs
2 tablespoons (30 ml) to 1 bottle of natural
  red food coloring
1 teaspoon (5 ml) vanilla extract
¾ cup + 2 tablespoons (200 ml) buttermilk
1 teaspoon (5 ml) white vinegar

FILLING AND TOPPING:
Mascarpone frosting (see recipe 6)
1¼ cups (300 ml) pecans
IN ADVANCE:
Line two 9-inch (23 cm) round cake pans.
Preheat oven to 350°F (180°C).

1	Sift the flour, salt and cocoa into a bowl and set aside.	2	Whisk the sugar and oil together in another bowl until well blended.	3	Add the eggs and mix again to combine.
4	Add the food coloring, vanilla, buttermilk and vinegar and blend well.	5	Add the flour mix and blend until well combined and there are no lumps.	6	Spoon the mix into the prepared pans. Bake for 25 to 30 minutes.

7 8
9 10

7	Allow the cakes to cool in the pans for 10 minutes, then turn out and cool completely on a wire rack.	8	Prepare the mascarpone frosting (see recipe 6). Sandwich the 2 cakes together with one-third of the frosting.
9	Spread the remaining frosting over the top and sides of the cake.	10	Chop the pecans roughly, leaving 15 whole to decorate the top.

| 11 | Coat the sides of the cake with the chopped pecans and decorate the top with the reserved whole pecans. | **VARIATION**
❈
For a delicious chocolate cake, omit the red food coloring and add an extra tablespoon (15 ml) of cocoa powder. |

LEMON MERINGUE LAYER CAKE

✦ SERVES 10 TO 12 • PREPARATION: 30 MINUTES • BAKING TIME: 1½ HOURS ✦

7 tablespoons (100 ml) butter, softened
½ cup (125 ml) granulated or superfine sugar
¾ cup (175 ml) self-rising flour
Finely grated zest of 2 lemons
Juice of ½ lemon
2 eggs

4 egg whites
1⅓ cups (325 ml) granulated or superfine sugar
1 teaspoon (5 ml) cream of tartar
1 teaspoon (5 ml) vinegar
1 cup (250 ml) ground almonds
Mascarpone frosting (see recipe 6)

⅔ cup (150 ml) lemon curd
2 tablespoons (30 ml) limoncello liqueur
1½ teaspoons (7 ml) flaked almonds
IN ADVANCE: Grease and line an 8-inch
(20 cm) round cake pan. Preheat oven to
350°F (180°C).

1	Mix butter, ½ cup (125 ml) of sugar, flour, half the almonds, half the zest, juice and eggs.	2	Spoon the mixture into the prepared pan.	3	Bake for 20 to 25 minutes, until well risen. Cool in pan; turn out onto rack.
4	Lower oven to 275°F (140°C). Beat egg whites until stiff and gradually beat in sugar.	5	Add the cream of tartar and vinegar at high speed. Fold in the ground almonds and remaining lemon zest.	6	Divide mix between 2 lined baking sheets. Spread into 8-inch (20 cm) rounds.

7	Bake for 60 minutes, until the paper peels away from the base of the meringue. Allow to cool on a wire rack.	8	For the filling, mix the lemon curd and limoncello. Prepare the mascarpone frosting (see recipe 6) in another bowl.
9	To assemble, cut the cake in half and place one of the halves on a plate. Spread on a quarter of the lemon curd, then a quarter of the frosting.	10	Put a meringue on top and spread more limoncello mix and frosting over. Repeat with another cake layer and finish with a meringue.

11 Spread the remaining frosting over the top, drizzle with the limoncello mix and scatter the flaked almonds overtop.

VARIATION
❋

As an alternative, you can use the meringue as a pudding. Serve with cream and fresh summer fruits for a great summer treat.

HUMMINGBIRD CAKE

✦ SERVES 14 TO 16 • PREPARATION: 30 MINUTES • BAKING TIME: 40 TO 45 MINUTES ✦

3 cups (750 ml) cake flour
2 teaspoons (10 ml) baking soda
1⅞ cups (450 ml) granulated or superfine sugar
½ teaspoon (2 ml) ground cinnamon
Pinch of salt
⅞ cup (200 ml) canned pineapple pieces

4 bananas
1½ cups (375 ml) pecans
1½ cups (375 ml) cups sunflower oil
4 eggs
FILLING AND GARNISH:
Mascarpone frosting (see recipe 6)

1 cup (250 ml) pecans, roughly chopped, some left whole to decorate
IN ADVANCE:
Grease and line two 9-inch (23 cm) round cake pans. Preheat oven to 350°F (180°C).

1	Sift flour and baking soda into a bowl. Add sugar, cinnamon and salt.	2	Whiz the canned pineapple in a small food processor until puréed.	3	Peel the bananas and roughly mash with a fork.
4	Using a sharp knife, chop the pecans finely.	5	Mix the oil, eggs, puréed pineapple, mashed bananas and chopped nuts together.	6	Add the flour mixture and mix. ➢

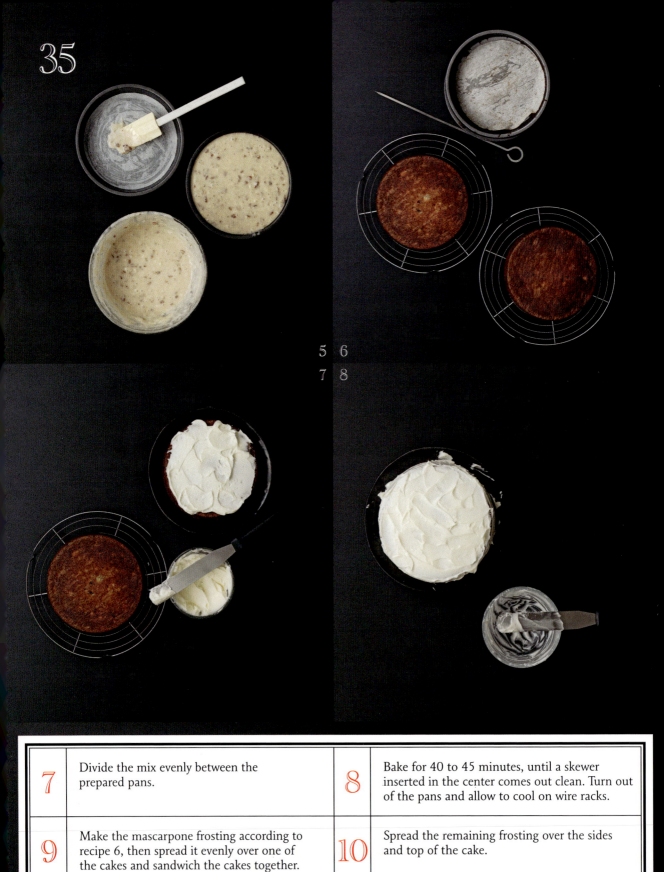

7	Divide the mix evenly between the prepared pans.	8	Bake for 40 to 45 minutes, until a skewer inserted in the center comes out clean. Turn out of the pans and allow to cool on wire racks.
9	Make the mascarpone frosting according to recipe 6, then spread it evenly over one of the cakes and sandwich the cakes together.	10	Spread the remaining frosting over the sides and top of the cake.

		VARIATION
		❋
11	Using your fingers, press the chopped pecans into the sides of the cake and arrange whole ones on the top.	Walnuts and hazelnuts also work well with this cake.

SOUR CREAM CAKE

❖ SERVES 8 TO 10 • PREPARATION: 15 MINUTES • BAKING TIME: 35 TO 40 MINUTES ❖

4 eggs
1 cup (250 ml) sour cream
1 teaspoon (5 ml) vanilla extract
1⅓ cups (325 ml) granulated or superfine
  sugar
2 cups (500 ml) self-rising flour

1 teaspoon (5 ml) baking powder
Small pinch of salt
Good pinch of ground cinnamon
FILLING AND TOPPING:
⅔ cup (150 ml) sour cream
7 tablespoons (100 ml) confectioners' sugar

½ vanilla bean, seeds scraped out
IN ADVANCE:
Grease and line an 8-inch (20 cm) round
cake pan. Preheat oven to 350°F (180°C).

1 2
3 4

1	Whisk the eggs, sour cream, vanilla and sugar together until well combined.	2	Sift the flour with the baking powder, salt and cinnamon into another bowl.
3	Mix the sour cream mixture and flour mixture together.	4	Pour the mix into the prepared pan and bake for 35 to 40 minutes. Turn out and allow to cool on a wire rack. ➤

		TIP
5	For the filling and topping, mix the sour cream, confectioners' sugar and vanilla seeds together until combined.	Use a couple of drops of vanilla extract instead of the vanilla seeds, if you like.

| 6 | Cut the cake in half and spread over some of the sour cream mix, then spread the sour cream mix over and top with fresh blueberries, if desired. | **TIP** ❋
 You could use crème fraîche to replace the sour cream in the cake and topping if you prefer. |

LOAF CAKES

4

SIMPLE CAKES

MOIST FRUIT CAKES

AROMATIC CAKES

HONEY CAKE

❧ SERVES 6 TO 8 • PREPARATION: 15 MINUTES • BAKING TIME: 35 TO 40 MINUTES ❧

5 tablespoons (75 ml) liquid honey
Finely grated zest and juice of 1 lemon
¾ cup unsalted butter, softened
⅔ cup + 2 tablespoons (175 ml) packed
  dark brown sugar
3 eggs

1⅓ cups (325 ml) self-rising flour
TO SERVE:
Mascarpone frosting (½ recipe; see recipe 6)
1 tablespoon (15 ml) honey

IN ADVANCE:
Grease and line an 8- by 4-inch (20 by 10 cm) loaf pan. Preheat oven to 350°F (180°C).
TIP: Cool in the pan for 10 minutes before turning out to cool on a wire rack.

| 1 | Heat the honey in a pan and add the lemon juice and zest. | 2 | Cream together the butter and brown sugar until light and fluffy. | 3 | Gradually beat in the eggs. |
| 4 | Sift in the flour, add the warm honey and mix well. | 5 | Spoon the mix into the prepared pan and smooth with a spoon. Bake for 35 to 40 minutes. Cool on wire rack. | 6 | Spread the icing evenly over the surface and drizzle the honey over the cake. |

MOLASSES CAKE

❧ SERVES 6 TO 8 • PREPARATION: 20 MINUTES • BAKING TIME: 60 MINUTES ❧

¾ cup (175 ml) unsalted butter, softened
⅔ cup + 2 tablespoons (200 ml) packed
    light brown sugar
3 tablespoons (45 ml) fancy molasses
3 eggs

3 cups (750 ml) self-rising flour
2 tablespoons (30 ml) milk
TO SERVE:
3 tablespoons (45 ml) fancy molasses
2 tablespoons (30 ml) dark rum

IN ADVANCE:
Line and grease a 9- by 5-inch (23 by 13 cm)
loaf pan. Preheat oven to 350°F (180°C).

1	Cream together the butter, brown sugar and molasses until light and fluffy.	2	Add the eggs and mix well.	3	Add the flour and milk to the mixture and blend well.
4	Spoon the mix into the prepared pan. Bake for 60 minutes. Leave for 5 to 10 minutes, then turn out and cool on a wire rack.	5	Gently warm the molasses and rum over low heat for 3 to 4 minutes, then allow to cool slightly.	6	Pour the warmed molasses mixture over the cake.

MADEIRA CAKE

❧ SERVES 6 TO 8 • PREPARATION: 15 MINUTES • BAKING TIME: 60 MINUTES ❧

¾ cup (175 ml) unsalted butter, softened
1⅓ cups (325 ml) granulated or
    superfine sugar
3 eggs
1⅔ cups (400 ml) self-rising flour
¾ cup (175 ml) ground almonds

Finely grated zest of 1 lemon
3 tablespoons (45 ml) milk
2 tablespoons (30 ml) chopped mixed peel
GARNISH:
2 tablespoons (30 ml) apricot jam

IN ADVANCE:
Grease and line an 8- by 4-inch
(20 by 10 cm) loaf pan. Preheat
oven to 350°F (180°C).

1
4

2
5

3
6

1	Cream the butter and sugar until light and fluffy.	2	Beat in the eggs one at a time, beating just until all the eggs are incorporated.	3	Sift in the flour, add the ground almonds, lemon zest and milk and mix.
4	Spoon the mix into the prepared pan. Bake for 30 minutes.	5	Take cake out of oven and top with mixed peel. Put back into oven and bake for 30 minutes. Cool in the pan.	6	Once cooled, take out of the pan and brush with apricot jam.

CHERRY & ALMOND CAKE

✦ SERVES 8 TO 10 • PREPARATION: 15 MINUTES • BAKING TIME: 55 TO 60 MINUTES ✦

1¾ cups (425 ml) candied cherries
⅞ cups (200 ml) unsalted butter, softened
1½ cups (375 ml) granulated or superfine
 sugar
1¼ cups (300 ml) self-rising flour

1¾ cups (375 ml) ground almonds
4 eggs
Finely grated zest of 2 lemons
1½ tablespoons (22 ml) flaked almonds
1½ tablespoons (22 ml) demerara sugar

IN ADVANCE:
Grease and line a 9- by 5-inch (23 by
13 cm) loaf pan. Preheat oven to 350ºF
(180ºC).

1	Slice the candied cherries in half and set aside.	2	Put all ingredients except flaked almonds, demerara and cherries into a bowl.	3	Beat the mixture for 3 to 4 minutes, until well combined.
4	Add the candied cherries to the mixture and fold through with a wooden spoon.	5	Spoon the mix into the prepared pan; sprinkle over the demerara and flaked almonds. Bake for 55 to 60 minutes.	6	Cool in the pan for 15 minutes, then turn out onto wire rack to cool slightly. Best served warm.

APPLE TEA CAKE

❧ SERVES 8 TO 10 • PREPARATION: 15 MINUTES • BAKING TIME: 60 MINUTES ❧

⅓ cup (75 ml) mixed dried fruit
¼ cup (60 ml) cooled breakfast tea
1 teaspoon (5 ml) ground ginger
⅞ cup (200 ml) unsalted butter, softened
3 eggs

1 cup (250 ml) packed light brown sugar
1⅔ cups (400 ml) self-rising flour
1 teaspoon (5 ml) baking powder
2 small red apples
Juice of ½ lemon

TOPPING:
3 tablespoons (45 ml) apricot jam
IN ADVANCE:
Grease and line a 9- by 5-inch (23 by 13 cm)
loaf pan. Preheat oven to 350°F (180°C).

1	Put the dried fruit, tea and half the ground ginger in a bowl and leave to soak for 20 minutes.	2	Melt the butter in a small pan and allow to cool.
3	Whisk the eggs and brown sugar together for about 3 minutes, until light.	4	Add the melted butter to the eggs along with the soaked fruit, flour and baking powder and mix until well combined.

5 6
7 8

5	Pour the cake mix into the prepared pan.	6	Core the apples and cut into thin slices. Toss the apples in lemon juice and the remaining ground ginger. Set aside.
7	Bake the cake for 30 minutes, then lay the apple slices over the top and bake for a further 30 minutes.	8	Allow the cake to cool in the pan for 20 minutes, then turn out onto a wire rack to cool completely.

| 9 | Once the cake is cooled, brush the top with apricot jam. | **TIP**
For a different taste, use Earl Grey or your favorite tea instead of ordinary breakfast tea. |

ORANGE MARMALADE CAKE

❧ SERVES 6 TO 8 • PREPARATION: 15 MINUTES • BAKING TIME: 50 TO 60 MINUTES ❧

½ cup (125 ml) marmalade (about one-third of a 16-ounce/454 g jar)
¾ cup (175 ml) unsalted butter, softened
¾ cup (175 ml) packed muscovado or light sugar

3 eggs, beaten
1¾ cups (425 ml) self-rising flour
½ teaspoon (2 ml) baking powder
2 teaspoons (10 ml) ground ginger
1 teaspoon (5 ml) pumpkin pie spices

IN ADVANCE:
Grease a 9- by 5-inch (23 by 13 cm) loaf pan and line with waxed or parchment paper. Preheat oven to 350°F (180°C).

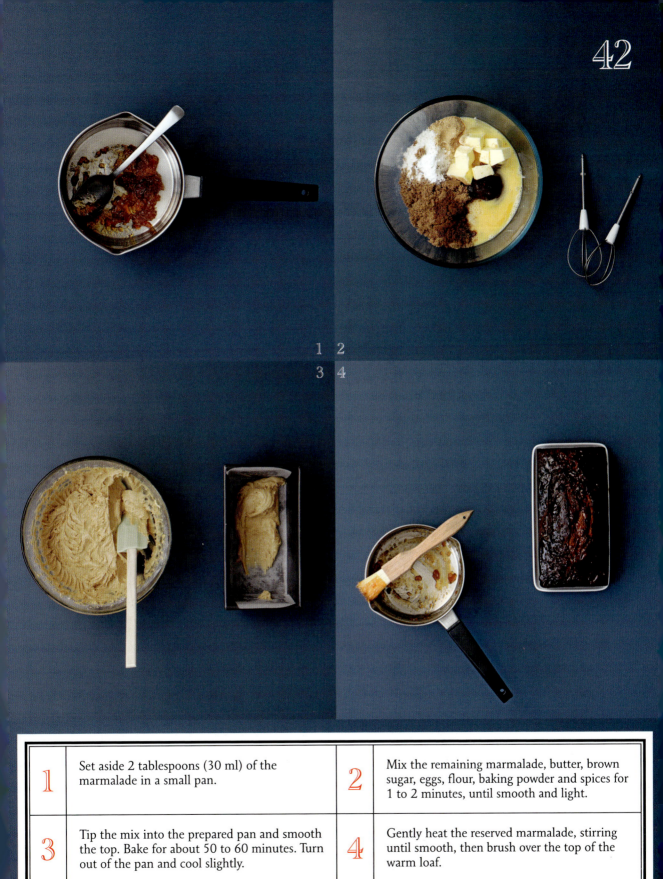

1	Set aside 2 tablespoons (30 ml) of the marmalade in a small pan.	2	Mix the remaining marmalade, butter, brown sugar, eggs, flour, baking powder and spices for 1 to 2 minutes, until smooth and light.
3	Tip the mix into the prepared pan and smooth the top. Bake for about 50 to 60 minutes. Turn out of the pan and cool slightly.	4	Gently heat the reserved marmalade, stirring until smooth, then brush over the top of the warm loaf.

ROSEMARY & LEMON CAKE

⇥ SERVES 6 • PREPARATION: 20 MINUTES • BAKING TIME: 50 TO 60 MINUTES ⇤

4 sprigs fresh rosemary
¾ cup (175 ml) butter, softened
¾ cup (175 ml) granulated or superfine sugar
3 eggs
1⅓ cup (325 ml) self-rising flour

2 tablespoons (30 ml) milk
Finely grated zest of 1 lemon
1 teaspoon (5 ml) vanilla extract
GLAZE:
Citrus glaze (½ recipe; see recipe 5)

IN ADVANCE:
Grease and line an 8- by 4-inch (20 by 10 cm) loaf pan. Preheat oven to 350°F (180°C).

1	Chop half the rosemary leaves, add to the butter and sugar and beat until light.	2	Gradually beat in the eggs, one at a time. Sift in a little flour to prevent curdling.	3	Sift in the flour with the milk, lemon zest and vanilla and beat well.
4	Pour into prepared pan and level top. Bake for 50 to 60 minutes. Leave for 10 minutes, then cool on a wire rack.	5	Spread the glaze on the top of the cake.	6	Decorate with the remaining rosemary leaves.

RHUBARB & CUSTARD CRUMBLE

❧ SERVES 8 TO 10 • PREPARATION: 15 MINUTES • BAKING TIME: 50 TO 55 MINUTES ❧

1¾ cups (425 ml) self-rising flour
2 tablespoons (30 ml) custard powder
⅓ cup (75 ml) semolina
⅔ cup (150 ml) granulated or superfine sugar
3 eggs
½ cup (125 ml) sunflower oil

1¾ ounces (50 g) preserved ginger,
   finely chopped
1 vanilla bean, seeds scraped out
3 tablespoons (45 ml) milk
¼ cup (60 ml) ricotta cheese
7 ounces (200 g) rhubarb, finely chopped

½ cup (125 ml) old-fashioned rolled oats
IN ADVANCE:
Grease and line a 9- by 5-inch (23 by
13 cm) loaf pan. Preheat oven to 325°F
(160°C).

1 2
3 4

1	Sift the flour and custard powder into a bowl and stir in the semolina and sugar.	2	Mix the eggs, oil, ginger, vanilla seeds, milk and ricotta together in another bowl.	
3	Add the oil mixture to the dry ingredients and whisk to combine.	4	Spoon two-thirds of the mix into the prepared pan, using the back of a spoon to press it down. Put the chopped rhubarb on top.	➢

		TIP
5	Loosely spread the remaining cake mix over the rhubarb and sprinkle with oats. Bake in the preheated oven for 50 to 55 minutes, until golden brown and cooked through. Allow to cool completely before removing from the pan.	Make sure to use a flavorless oil such as vegetable or sunflower when making this cake, as other oils can be quite strong and may ruin the finished flavor.

6

Slice the cake and serve with hot custard, if desired.

VARIATION
❊

For a brighter pink color in this cake, use the lovely forced rhubarb when in season.

BANANA & MAPLE SYRUP CAKE

❧ SERVES 8 TO 10 • PREPARATION: 15 MINUTES • BAKING TIME: 50 TO 55 MINUTES ❧

7 tablespoons (100 ml) unsalted butter,
  softened
1¾ cups (425 ml) self-rising flour
2 ripe bananas
Finely grated zest of 1 orange
½ teaspoon (2 ml) ground cinnamon

½ cups (125 ml) granulated or superfine sugar
2 eggs
1 cup (500 ml) walnut pieces
½ cups (125 ml) quick-cooking rolled oats
6 tablespoons (90 ml) pure maple syrup
½ banana, sliced lengthwise

TOPPING:
2 tablespoons (30 ml) pure maple syrup
Brown sugar, for sprinkling
IN ADVANCE: Lightly grease and line the
base of a 9- by 5-inch (23 by 13 cm) loaf pan.
Preheat oven to 350ºF (180ºC).

1	Rub the butter into the flour until the mixture resembles fine crumbs.	2	Peel and mash the bananas, then stir into the flour mixture.	3	Add the zest, cinnamon, sugar, eggs, walnuts, oats and maple syrup and beat.
4	Pour mix into prepared pan. Bake for 20 minutes. Put the ½ banana on top and bake for 30 to 35 minutes.	5	Gently warm the maple syrup in a pan, then brush over the cooled cake.	6	To finish, sprinkle some brown sugar over the top of the cake.

CANDIED PEEL CAKE

❧ SERVES 6 TO 8 • PREPARATION: 20 MINUTES • BAKING TIME: 60 TO 70 MINUTES ❧

⅔ cup (150 ml) unsalted butter, softened
Pinch of salt
½ cup (125 ml) packed muscovado or light
   brown sugar
3 eggs
1⅓ cups (325 ml) self-rising flour

7 ounces (200 g) good-quality Italian
   candied peel
1⅓ cup (325 ml) raisins
¼ cup (60 ml) pine nuts
GARNISH:
2 tablespoons (30 ml) unsalted butter

¼ cup (60 ml) granulated or superfine sugar
4 tablespoons (60 ml) Grand Marnier
IN ADVANCE:
Lightly grease and line the base of a 9- by
5-inch (23 by 13 cm) loaf pan. Preheat
oven to 315°F (160°C).

1	Beat the butter, salt, sugar, eggs and flour until well blended.	2	Add the candied peel and raisins and mix well.	3	Pour mix into prepared pan; sprinkle pine nuts on top. Bake for 60 to 70 minutes. Cool slightly.
4	Meanwhile, gently heat the butter and sugar until the sugar has dissolved and become slightly golden.	5	Leave over a low heat and add the Grand Marnier. Simmer for 2 to 3 minutes, until thick.	6	Allow the syrup to cool slightly, then brush over the cooled cake.

CARDAMOM & ORANGE CAKE

❧ SERVES 6 TO 8 • PREPARATION: 15 MINUTES • BAKING TIME: 40 MINUTES ❧

¾ cup (175 ml) unsalted butter, softened
¾ cup (175 ml) granulated or superfine
   sugar
Finely grated zest and juice of 1 orange
3 eggs
⅓ cup (75 ml) semolina

1¼ cups (300 ml) self-rising flour
Pinch of salt
½ teaspoon (2 ml) ground green cardamom,
   plus extra for topping
TOPPING:
1 orange, thinly sliced

Orange syrup (see recipe 7)
IN ADVANCE:
Grease and line an 8- by 4-inch (20 by
10 cm) loaf pan. Preheat oven to 350°F
(180°C).

1	Cream the butter and sugar together until light and fluffy.	2	Mix in orange zest and juice. Add eggs one at a time, beating after each addition.	3	Add the dry ingredients and mix well.
4	Pour the mix into the prepared pan. Bake for 30 minutes, then arrange 6 to 8 slices of orange on top.	5	Bake for a further 10 minutes. Leave for 10 minutes before turning out and cooling on a wire rack.	6	Make the syrup according to recipe 7 and brush it over the cake. Sprinkle with ground cardamom.

GINGER LOAF CAKE

➤ SERVES 8 TO 10 • PREPARATION: 20 MINUTES • BAKING TIME: 35 TO 40 MINUTES ⬅

⅓ cup (75 ml) honey
2 ounces (55 g) preserved ginger, chopped plus
    2 tablespoons (30 ml) syrup
½ cup (125 ml) unsalted butter, softened
2 teaspoons (10 ml) ground ginger
2 heaped tablespoons (30 ml) raisins
Pinch of salt

½ cup + 2 tablespoons (280 ml) packed dark
    muscovado or brown sugar
3 large eggs
1 cup (250 ml) milk
2 cups (500 ml) self-rising flour
½ teaspoon (2 ml) ground cinnamon
1 teaspoon (5 ml) baking soda

GARNISH:
Orange buttercream (½ recipe; see recipe 3)
1 ounce (30 g) preserved ginger, sliced
IN ADVANCE:
Grease and line a 9- by 5-inch (23 by 13 cm)
loaf pan. Preheat oven to 350ºF (180ºC).

1	Heat honey, syrup, butter, ground ginger, chopped ginger, raisins, salt and sugar.	2	Put the eggs in a bowl, add the milk and beat gently to combine.	3	Combine the butter mixture with the dry ingredients and eggs. Mix well.
4	Pour the mix into the prepared pan. Bake for 35 to 40 minutes. Allow to cool for 10 minutes before turning out.	5	Make the buttercream according to recipe 3 and spread it over the cake.	6	To finish, sprinkle over slices of preserved ginger.

HONEY SPICE CAKE

✦ SERVES 6 TO 8 • PREPARATION: 30 MINUTES • BAKING TIME: 40 TO 45 MINUTES ✦

⅓ cup (75 ml) thick honey
½ cup (125 ml) packed dark brown sugar
1 teaspoon (5 ml) ground cinnamon
1 whole star anise
½ teaspoon (2 ml) ground ginger
⅓ cup + 2 tablespoons (100 ml) boiling water
¼ cup (60 ml) ginger wine

2 cups (500 ml) cake flour
1 teaspoon (5 ml) baking powder
1 egg
1 tablespoon (15 ml) fancy molasses
½ cup (125 ml) mixed dried fruit
¼–⅓ cup (60–75 ml) chopped crystallized ginger

TO SERVE:
4 tablespoons (60 ml) thick dark honey
IN ADVANCE:
Grease an 8- by 4-inch (20 by 10 cm) loaf pan. Preheat oven to 300°F(150°C).

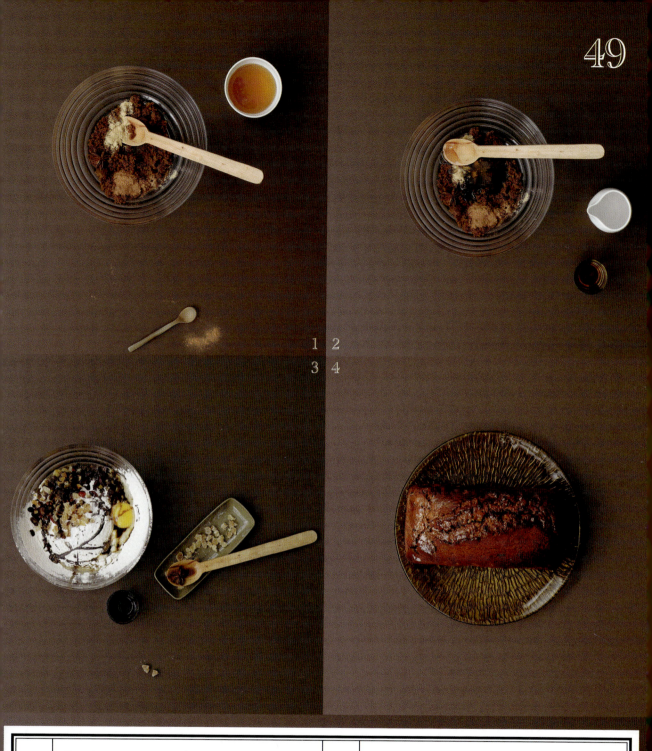

1	Put the honey, sugar, cinnamon, star anise and ginger in a heatproof bowl.	2	Pour in the boiling water and add the ginger wine. Stir and allow to cool for 15 minutes. Remove the star anise.
3	Sift the flour and baking powder into the cooled mix. Add the egg, molasses, dried fruit and crystallized ginger and mix well.	4	Spoon the mix into the prepared pan. Bake for 1 hour. Cool slightly on a wire rack, then brush with the honey. Serve warm.

CHOCOLATE CAKES

5

RICH CHOCOLATE CAKES

CHOCOLATE & SPICE CAKES

CLASSIC CHOCOLATE CAKES

BLACK FOREST CAKE

❧ SERVES 10 TO 12 • PREPARATION: 40 MINUTES • BAKING TIME: 30 TO 35 MINUTES ❧

6 eggs
¾ cup (175 ml) granulated or superfine sugar
7 tablespoons (100 ml) good-quality cocoa powder
¼ teaspoon (1 ml) baking powder
Small pinch of salt

1 cup (250 ml) self-rising flour
2 cups (500 ml) whipping cream (36%)
½ cup (125 ml) kirsch cherry liqueur
⅓– ½ cup (75–125 ml) good-quality black cherry jam
7 ounces (200 g) fresh pitted cherries

GARNISH:
Dark chocolate curls (see recipe 8)
1¾ ounces (50 g) whole cherries
½ cup (125 ml) toasted flaked almonds
IN ADVANCE:
Grease and line a 9-inch (23 cm) round cake pan. Preheat oven to 350ºF (180ºC).

1	Beat the eggs and sugar together for 5 to 7 minutes, until pale and thick.	**2**	Sift the cocoa powder, baking powder, salt and flour together.	**3**	Fold the cocoa mixture into the eggs.
4	Carefully spoon the mix into the prepared pan. Bake for 30 to 35 minutes, until the sponge is well risen.	**5**	Turn the cooked cake out onto a wire rack and allow to cool.	**6**	For the filling, whip the cream until thick. ➤

5   6
7   8

7	Using a long, sharp serrated knife, cut the cooled cake into 3 layers.	8	Starting with the bottom layer, spoon over 2 tablespoons (30 ml) kirsch, spread over half the jam, a sprinkle of cherries and a quarter of the cream.
9	Top with a second layer of cake and repeat step 8. Repeat again with the third sponge layer, then brush over any remaining kirsch.	10	Spread the remaining cream around the sides of the cake and cover it with the toasted almonds.

	Decorate the top of the cake with chocolate curls and whole cherries.	**TIP** ❋
11		Use canned cherries if fresh ones are not available

CHERRY & CHOCOLATE CAKE

❖ SERVES 8 TO 10 • PREPARATION: 20 MINUTES • BAKING TIME: 20 TO 25 MINUTES ❖

7 ounces (200 g) dark chocolate, chopped
⅔ cup (150 ml) unsalted butter, softened
   and cut into small pieces
⅔ cup (150 ml) kirsch cherry liqueur
½ cup (125 ml) ground almonds
Pinch of salt

¾ cup (175 ml) self-rising flour
4 eggs
⅔ cup (150 ml) granulated or superfine sugar
TOPPING:
⅓ cup (75 ml) good-quality cherry jam
2 tablespoons (30 ml) kirsch cherry liqueur

GARNISH:
Chocolate curls (see recipe 8)
3 ounces (80 g) fresh cherries
IN ADVANCE:
Grease and line an 8-inch (20 cm) springform
pan. Preheat oven to 350°F (180°C).

1 2
3 4

1	Melt the chocolate and butter in a heatproof bowl set over a pan of simmering water. Allow to cool slightly. Add the cherry liqueur and mix.	2	Stir in the ground almonds and salt, then sift in the flour.	
3	Beat the eggs and sugar in a clean bowl for 5 minutes, until pale and light.	4	Using a metal spoon, fold the egg mixture into the chocolate mixture.	➤

5	Spoon the mix into the prepared pan and arrange some of the fresh cherries on top. Bake for 20 to 25 minutes, until set but slightly soft in the center.	6	Allow the cake to cool for 10 minutes in the pan, then turn it out onto a wire rack and allow to cool completely.
7	Heat the cherry jam and kirsch together in a small pan.	8	Brush the warmed jam mixture over the top of the cake.

9 Decorate with chocolate curls and the remaining fresh cherries.

TIP
❀

If there is any cake left, store in an airtight container for 2 to 3 days.

PRALINE CRUNCH CAKE

❧ SERVES 10 TO 12 • PREPARATION: 20 MINUTES • BAKING TIME: 30 TO 35 MINUTES ❧

PRALINE:
½ cup (125 ml) granulated or superfine sugar
1 cup (250 ml) hazelnuts

CAKE:
7 ounces (200 g) dark chocolate (70% cocoa)
⅞ cup (200 ml) unsalted butter, softened

⅔ cup (150 ml) packed light brown sugar
4 eggs
1⅔ cups (400 ml) cake flour
1 teaspoon (5 ml) baking powder
Pinch of salt
3 tablespoons (45 ml) hazelnut praline

FILLING AND TOPPING:
Orange buttercream (see recipe 3)
5 tablespoons (75 ml) crushed hazelnut
   praline

IN ADVANCE:
Grease and line an 8-inch (20 cm) round
cake pan. Preheat oven to 350°F (180°C).

1 2
3 4

For praline, put sugar in a shallow non-stick frying pan. Scatter over the nuts and set over a low heat until the sugar turns a caramel color.	*2*	When the caramel has turned a deep brown, pour onto a rimmed baking sheet lined with parchment paper and cool. Crush in a food processor.	
Break the chocolate into pieces, put it in a heatproof bowl and melt over a pan of simmering water. Allow to cool slightly.	*4*	Mix the butter, brown sugar, eggs, flour, baking powder, salt and 3 tablespoons (45 ml) of pralines until well combined.	➤

5	Add the melted chocolate to the cake mixture.	6	Spoon the mix into the prepared pan. Bake for 30 to 35 minutes. Turn the cake out on a wire rack to cool completely.
7	Make the buttercream according to recipe 3. Cut the cake in half and sandwich the cake together with some of the buttercream.	8	Spread the top and sides of the cake with the remaining buttercream.

9	Cover the sides of the cake with crushed praline and then sprinkle the remaining praline over the top	**TIP** ✳ As an alternative to buttercream, use the same amount of whipped cream.

CHOCOLATE BROWNIE CAKE

❧ SERVES 12 TO 14 • PREPARATION: 30 MINUTES • BAKING TIME: 25 TO 30 MINUTES ❧

7 ounces (200 g) dark chocolate, chopped
⅔ cup (150 ml) butter, softened
⅔ cup (150 ml) brown sugar
3 eggs
½ cup (125 ml) self-rising flour

Small pinch of salt
3½ ounces (100 g) marshmallows, cut in half
3½ ounces (100 g) pecans, chopped
3½ ounces (100 g) white chocolate, chopped

GARNISH:
½ cup (125 ml) chocolate-hazelnut spread
Marshmallow flowers (see recipe 9)

IN ADVANCE:
Grease and line a 9-inch (23 cm) round cake pan. Preheat oven to 350°F (180°C).

1 Put the dark chocolate and butter in a heatproof bowl set over a pan of simmering water and leave until melted.	**2** Using an electric mixer, beat the brown sugar and eggs in another bowl for about 2 to 4 minutes, until light and fluffy.
3 Mix the melted chocolate into the sugar mixture.	**4** Sift the flour and salt and fold into the mixture with a metal spoon, trying to retain as much of the air as possible. ➢

5	Add the marshmallows, pecans and white chocolate.	6	Pour the mix into the prepared pan. Bake for 25 to 30 minutes, until a skewer inserted in the center comes out slightly gooey.
7	Allow the cake to cool in the pan for 10 minutes before turning out onto a wire rack to cool.	8	Using a palette knife, spread the chocolate-hazelnut spread over top of the cake.

9 Decorate with the marshmallow flowers.

VARIATION
❋

For a change, replace the pecans with the same amount of chocolate cookie pieces.

WHITE CHOCOLATE CAKE

❖ SERVES 8 TO 10 • PREPARATION: 15 MINUTES • BAKING TIME: 30 MINUTES ❖

2 eggs
⅞ cup (200 ml) granulated or superfine sugar
7 tablespoons (100 ml) unsalted butter, melted
Finely grated zest of 1 lemon
Juice of ½ lemon

¾ cup (175 ml) self-rising flour
½ cup (125 ml) ground almonds

TOPPING:
1¾ ounces (50 g) white chocolate, chopped
3½ ounces (100 g) blueberries (about ⅔ cup/150 ml)

GARNISH:
White chocolate curls (see recipe 8)

IN ADVANCE:
Grease and line the base of an 8-inch (20 cm) round cake pan. Preheat oven to 350°F (180°C).

1	Mix the eggs and sugar together until creamy.	2	Add the butter and lemon zest and juice and mix until combined.	
3	Sift in the flour, add ground almonds and mix well, until everything is combined.	4	Spoon the mix into the prepared pan and lightly arrange the chopped white chocolate and blueberries on top of the cake.	➤

| 5 | Bake for 30 minutes, until well risen and the cake springs back when touched gently on the top. Leave in the pan for a few minutes, then turn out onto a wire rack and cool completely. | **TIP**
✳
Place the cake on the middle rack of the oven to ensure even browning during baking. |

6 Decorate the cake with chocolate curls.

VARIATION
❋
You can replace the blueberries with fresh raspberries, if you prefer.

BEET CHOCOLATE CAKE

❧ SERVES 6 TO 8 • PREPARATION: 20 MINUTES • BAKING TIME: 40 TO 45 MINUTES ❧

7 tablespoons (100 ml) cocoa powder
1½ cups (375 ml) cake flour
1½ teaspoons (7 ml) baking powder
Pinch of salt
1⅓ cups (325 ml) granulated or
    superfine sugar

12 ounces (350 g) fresh beets, peeled
3 eggs
¾ cup (175 ml) sunflower oil
1 teaspoon (5 ml) vanilla extract

GARNISH:
Mascarpone frosting (½ recipe; see recipe 6)
Cocoa powder
IN ADVANCE:
Grease and line an 8-inch (20 cm) round
cake pan. Preheat oven to 350°F (180°C).

1	Sift the cocoa, flour, baking powder and salt into a bowl. Add the sugar.	2	Chop the beets and whiz in a food processor until smooth.	3	Add the eggs, oil and vanilla and whiz until blended.
4	Mix in the dry ingredients and blend. Pour the mix into the prepared pan.	5	Bake for 40 to 45 minutes. Cool for 10 minutes. Turn out and put upside down on a wire rack to cool.	6	Make the frosting according to recipe 6 and spread over the cake, then dust with cocoa powder.

GINGER CHOCOLATE CAKE

❧ SERVES 10 TO 12 • PREPARATION: 20 MINUTES • BAKING TIME: 25 MINUTES ❧

7 ounces (200 g) gingersnap cookies
¼ cup (60 ml) unsalted butter, melted
7 ounces (200 g) dark chocolate, chopped
⅞ cup (200 ml) unsalted butter
4 eggs
1 cup (250 ml) granulated or superfine sugar

Pinch of salt
1¼ cups (300 ml) self-rising flour
1 tablespoon (15 ml) cocoa powder
½ cup (125 ml) candied ginger, chopped
GARNISH:
Chocolate ganache (see recipe 4)

¼ cup (60 ml) candied ginger, chopped
1 ounce (30 g) honeycomb, smashed
IN ADVANCE:
Grease and line an 8-inch (20 cm) springform pan. Preheat oven to 350°F (180°C).

1	Blitz the cookies to fine crumbs. Stir in the butter and spread in pan. Let set.	2	Melt the chocolate and butter as in recipe 53. Let cool for 3 minutes.	3	Add the eggs, sugar, salt, flour, cocoa and ginger and mix well.
4	Scrape mix into the prepared pan. Bake for 25 to 30 minutes. Leave for 15 minutes. Take out of pan and cool on a wire rack.	5	Make the ganache according to recipe 4 and spread it over the cake.	6	Decorate with the chopped ginger and honeycomb.

MINT CHOCOLATE CHIP CAKE

❖ SERVES 10 TO 12 • PREPARATION: 15 TO 20 MINUTES • BAKING TIME: 25 TO 30 MINUTES, PLUS CHILLING TIME ❖

7 ounces (200g) chocolate-covered
   digestive cookies
2 tablespoons (30 ml) unsalted butter, melted
¼ teaspoon (1 ml) peppermint extract
3½ ounces (100g) chocolate covered
   mint patties

3½ ounces (100g) dark chocolate (70% cocoa)
⅔ cup (150 ml) unsalted butter, softened
⅔ cup (150 ml) packed light brown sugar
3 eggs
1¼ cups (300 ml) self-rising flour, sifted
Pinch of salt

GARNISH:
3½ ounces (100g) chocolate mint patties
3 tablespoons (45 ml) milk
Bronze-colored edible glitter
IN ADVANCE:
Lightly oil a 9-inch (23 cm) round cake pan.
Preheat oven to 350ºF (180ºC).

1	Whiz the cookies into crumbs in a food processor or by placing them in a plastic bag and gently smashing with a rolling pin.	2	Stir in the melted butter and peppermint extract. Put the cookie mixture into the prepared pan, spreading into the corners. Chill.
3	Melt the mint patties, chocolate and butter in a heatproof bowl over a pan of simmering water. Cool for 5 minutes.	4	Mix the brown sugar and eggs together in a large bowl until frothy.

5 6
7 8

5	Blend in the chocolate mixture and gently fold in the sifted flour and salt with a metal spoon.	6	Pour the mix on top of the base. Bake for 25 to 30 minutes, until the cake feels a little spongy to the touch. Cool, then chill for 60 minutes.	
7	For the garnish, melt the mint patties as in step 3. Add the milk and allow to cool slightly.	8	Using a palette knife, spread the cold chocolate-mint mixture on top of the cake, then chill until set.	➤

	To finish, dust the cake with some bronze-colored edible glitter.	Dust with your favorite edible glitter, which comes in many amazing colors.

INDIAN SPICES CHOC CAKE

✦ SERVES 8 TO 10 • PREPARATION: 20 MINUTES • BAKING TIME: 20 TO 25 MINUTES, PLUS CHILLING TIME ✦

¼ teaspoon (1 ml) ground cinnamon
Good pinch of crushed red pepper flakes
¼ teaspoon (1 ml) whole black peppercorns
¼ teaspoon (1 ml) ground cardamom
10 ounces (300g) dark chocolate
   (70% cocoa), chopped

½ teaspoon (2 ml) vanilla extract
1 tablespoon (15 ml) brandy
Pinch of salt
7 tablespoons (100 ml) unsalted butter, softened
3 eggs
¾ cup (75 ml) granulated or superfine sugar

⅔ cup (150 ml) self-rising flour
GARNISH:
Gold edible glitter
IN ADVANCE:
Grease and line an 8-inch (20 cm) springform
cake pan. Preheat oven to 350ºF (180ºC).

1	Whiz the spices in a spice grinder or clean coffee grinder until fine.	2	Melt chocolate, vanilla, brandy, spices, salt and butter as in recipe 53.	3	Beat the eggs and sugar in a clean bowl until light.
4	Fold the egg mixture and flour into the slightly cooled chocolate mixture.	5	Pour the mix into the prepared pan. Bake for 20 to 25 minutes. Cool, then chill for a further 1 hour.	6	To decorate, brush with gold edible glitter before cutting into slices.

NYC BLACKOUT CAKE

❄ SERVES 14 TO 16 • PREPARATION: 60 MINUTES • BAKING TIME: 30 MINUTES PLUS CHILLING TIME ❄

2 cups (500 ml) milk
2⅔ cups (750 ml) granulated or superfine sugar
½ teaspoon (2 ml) salt
5 tablespoons (45 ml) cornstarch
6 ounces (170 g) dark chocolate, chopped
¼ cup (60 ml) unsalted butter, melted

⅓ cup + 2 tablespoons (100 ml) vegetable oil
3 eggs
2 teaspoons (10 ml) vanilla extract
7 tablespoons (100 ml) cocoa powder
1 tablespoon (15 ml) baking powder
¾ cup (175 ml) strong brewed coffee

1⅔ cups (400 ml) self-rising flour
¾ cup + 2 tablespoons (200 ml) buttermilk
IN ADVANCE:
Oil two 9-inch (23 cm) round cake pans.
Preheat oven to 350°F (180°C).

1	Make a chocolate cream: Bring the milk, half the sugar, the salt and cornstarch to a boil, whisking occasionally, until the sugar dissolves.	2	Add the dark chocolate and return the mixture to a boil, whisking constantly. Leave on the heat, whisking until very thick, for 3 to 4 minutes.
3	Pour into a bowl and allow to cool for 2 to 3 minutes. Cover with plastic wrap and chill for about 45 minutes, until firm.	4	In a stand mixer, mix the butter, remaining sugar and oil until light.

5 6
7 8

5	Add the eggs and mix well.	6	With the mixer running at low speed, add the vanilla, cocoa powder, baking powder and coffee and mix well.
7	Sift in the flour, then add the buttermilk and mix until combined.	8	Pour mix into prepared pans. Bake for 30 to 35 minutes. Cool in pans for 15 minutes, then turn out onto wire racks to cool.

When cooled, using a long serrated knife, cut the cakes in half horizontally. Reserve 3 halves of the cake.

TIPS

As an alternative, use crushed chocolate sandwich cookies for the topping.

After baking the cakes, don't turn the oven off, as you will need to bake the topping.

10 11
12 13

10	Break the remaining half-cake into large crumbs and bake for a further 20 minutes, until crunchy.	**11**	To build the cake, put a cake layer on a serving plate (reserving the most even layer for the top) and spread with the cooled chocolate cream.
12	Top with another layer of cake, then chocolate cream, then the final layer of cake.	**13**	Cover the top and sides of the cake with the remaining chocolate cream.

14   Chill for at least 2 hours, then press the cake crumbs on top of the cake.

TIP
❋

This cake is best eaten the same day it is made.

RICH CHOCOLATE MUD CAKE

❧ SERVES 12 TO 14 • PREPARATION: 40 MINUTES • BAKING TIME: 60 MINUTES ❧

⅓ cup (75 ml) unsalted butter, softened
7 ounces (200g) dark chocolate sandwich cookies
FILLING:
14 ounces (400g) dark chocolate, broken into
    pieces

¾ cup + 3 tablespoons (225 ml) unsalted
    butter, softened
⅓ cup (75 ml) strong brewed coffee
1¼ cups (300 ml) light cream (20%)
1¼ cups (300 ml) dark brown or muscovado sugar
Pinch of salt

6 eggs
⅓ cup + 1 tablespoon (90 ml) cake flour
2 teaspoons (10 ml) vanilla extract
IN ADVANCE:
Grease and line a 9-inch (23 cm) round cake
pan. Preheat oven to 325°F (160°C).

1	Melt the butter in a small pan and cool slightly.	2	Whiz the cookies in a blender to a crumb consistency.	3	Add the melted butter to the cookie crumbs and mix well.
4	Spoon the crumb mix into the prepared pan and level with the back of a metal spoon. Chill for 20 minutes.	5	For the filling, melt the chocolate, butter and coffee as in recipe 53. Allow to cool.	6	Mix the cream, brown sugar, salt, eggs, flour and vanilla into to the chocolate mix. ➤

| 7 | Pour the mix onto the base. Bake for 1 hour. Allow to cool in the pan before turning out onto a serving plate. | **TIP**
✳
For a boozy alternative, replace the brewed coffee with the same amount of bourbon. |

		TIP
	Serve the cake with whipped cream, if desired.	This recipe also works well with other filled cookies instead of the chocolate sandwich cookies.
8		

FLOURLESS CHOCOLATE CAKE

❧ SERVES 10 TO 12 • PREPARATION: 20 MINUTES • BAKING TIME: 35 TO 40 MINUTES ❦

1 pound (500 g) dark chocolate (70% cocoa), broken into pieces
¾ cup (175 ml) unsalted butter, softened
5 eggs, separated
1⅓ cups + 2 tablespoons (350 ml) granulated or superfine sugar

1 cup (250 ml) ground almonds
Pinch of salt
GARNISH:
Cocoa powder
Gold edible glitter

IN ADVANCE:
Grease and line a 9-inch (23 cm) round cake pan. Preheat oven to 350ºF (180ºC).

1 2
3 4

1	Melt the chocolate and butter in a heatproof bowl set over a pan of simmering water. Allow to cool slightly.	2	Whisk the egg yolks and sugar in another bowl for 2 to 3 minutes, until light and creamy.	
3	Whisk the egg whites in a clean bowl until soft peaks form.	4	Fold the egg yolk mixture into the melted chocolate.	➤

| 5 | Using a large metal spoon, gently fold in the ground almonds, salt and egg whites. Spoon the mix into the prepared pan. Bake for 35 to 40 minutes, until a skewer inserted into the center comes out clean. | **TIP**
❋
This is a wonderful, moist, gluten-free chocolate cake. |

6 Allow the cake to cool slightly, then dust with cocoa powder and gold edible glitter and serve.

TIP
❋

Use the same mixture to make 12 to 14 cupcakes, if you like.

CHEESECAKES

6

BAKED CHEESECAKES

FRUIT CHEESECAKES

NO-BAKE CHEESECAKES

CLASSIC NYC CHEESECAKE

❧ SERVES 10 TO 12 • PREPARATION: 15 MINUTES • BAKING TIME: 60 MINUTES, PLUS CHILLING TIME ❧

7 ounces (200 g) digestive cookies
¼ cup (60 ml) unsalted butter, melted
⅓ cup (75 ml) cornstarch
1 tablespoon (15 ml) lemon juice
Finely grated zest of ½ lemon
1 teaspoon (5 ml) vanilla extract

1½ pounds (750 g) cream cheese, softened
1 cup (250 ml) granulated or superfine sugar
⅓ cup + 2 tablespoons (100 ml) heavy cream (36%)
2 eggs + 1 egg yolk
TO SERVE:
1 cup (250 ml) strawberries

1 cup (250 ml) blackberries
IN ADVANCE:
Grease sides of a 9-inch (23 cm) removable-bottom or springform pan and double-wrap it in foil. Preheat oven to 300°F (150°C).

1	Crush the cookies into fine crumbs in a food processor or by putting them in a plastic bag and gently bashing with a rolling pin.	**2**	Put the crushed cookies in a bowl and mix in the melted butter.
3	Spread the cookie mixture over the base of the prepared pan with a spoon, pressing it down to get it right to the edges. Chill.	**4**	Beat the cornstarch, lemon juice and zest, vanilla and cream cheese until smooth, gradually adding the sugar. Add the cream. ➤

5 6
7

5	Add the eggs and yolk, one at a time, mixing well after each addition.	6	Pour the cheese mix over the chilled cookie crust (tap the pan on the counter to remove any bubbles).
7	Bake in a water bath with 1 inch (2.5 cm) of warm water for 1 hour. It should have a slight wobble. Cool in the water for 45 minutes.	8	Remove from water bath and chill for 3 hours before serving. Carefully remove from the pan and transfer to a serving dish.

 9 Serve the cheesecake with fresh strawberries and raspberries.

TIP
❋

By using a water bath, you will prevent your cheesecake from cracking.

SQUASH CHEESECAKE

❧ SERVES 10 TO 12 • PREPARATION: 40 MINUTES • BAKING TIME: 40 TO 50 MINUTES, PLUS CHILLING TIME ❧

SQUASH PUREE:
1 pound (500 g) butternut squash, cut
   in half and seeded

CRUST:
7 ounces (200 g) ginger cookies
¼ cup (60 ml) unsalted butter, melted

CHEESECAKE:
½ cup (125 ml) packed light brown sugar
¼ teaspoon (1 ml) ground cinnamon
14 ounces (400 g) cream cheese
3 eggs
1 teaspoon (5 ml) vanilla extract
⅔ cup (150 ml) buttermilk

GARNISH:
2 tablespoons (30 ml) green pumpkin seeds,
toasted

IN ADVANCE:
Grease an 8-inch (20 cm) springform pan.
Preheat oven to 325°F (160°C).

1	Bake the squash until soft. Cool, then purée the flesh in a food processor.	2	Whiz the ginger cookies to fine crumbs and add the melted butter.	3	Press the mixture into the base of the prepared pan. Cover and chill.
4	Mix the brown sugar, cinnamon and cream cheese together in a bowl until smooth.	5	Add the eggs, vanilla, squash puree and buttermilk and mix well. Pour filling over the crust.	6	Bake for 40 to 50 minutes. Cool in oven for 5 minutes, with door ajar; cool and chill. Scatter seeds over.

PRALINE CHEESECAKE

❧ SERVES 10 TO 12 • PREPARATION: 30 MINUTES • BAKING TIME: 40 TO 50 MINUTES, PLUS COOLING TIME ❧

½ cup (125 ml) granulated or superfine sugar
4 ounces (100 g) whole almonds, ½–⅔ cups
    (125–150 ml)
6 ounces (175 g) digestive cookies
⅓ cup (75 ml) unsalted butter
1 pound (450 g) cream cheese

2½ tablespoons (37 ml) cornstarch
7 ounces (200 g) mascarpone cheese
⅓ cup (75 ml) liquid honey
1 teaspoon (5 ml) vanilla extract
2 eggs + 1 egg yolk
3 tablespoons (45 ml) almond praline

GARNISH:
4 tablespoons (60 ml) crushed almond praline
IN ADVANCE:
Grease sides of a 9-inch (23 cm) springform
pan and double-wrap it in foil. Preheat oven
to 300ºF (150ºC).

1 2
3 4

1	For the praline, put sugar in a shallow non-stick frying pan and scatter in almonds. Set over low heat until sugar turns a caramel color.	2	When the caramel has turned a deep brown, pour the mixture onto a baking sheet lined with parchment paper and allow mixture to cool.
3	Crush the praline in a food processor until the mixture becomes gritty.	4	Whiz the cookies in a food processor until they're fine crumbs. Add the melted butter with ⅓ cup (75 ml) of the praline and mix. ➤

5

Spread the mixture evenly over the base of the prepared pan and press down gently to get it right to the edges. Chill for 15 to 20 minutes.

TIP

If you don't want to use the praline, try using honeycomb instead — it still gives you that lovely golden color but not the crunch.

6

Beat the cream cheese, cornstarch, mascarpone, honey, vanilla, eggs and egg yolk together in a bowl until smooth and creamy.

TIP
✳

After pouring the cheese mixture into the pan, tap the pan on the counter to remove any bubbles.

7 8
9 10

7	Pour the cheese mixture over the chilled cookie crust.	8	Scatter 3 tablespoons (45 ml) of crushed pralines over the top.
9	Bake in a water bath with 1 inch (2.5 cm) of warm water for 1 hour. It should have a slight wobble. Cool in the water for 45 minutes.	10	Cool completely in the pan for 1 to 2 hours, then run a knife around the edge to loosen and carefully remove the cheesecake from the pan.

11   Sprinkle over the remaining crushed praline and serve. The cheesecake is best served at room temperature.

Any remaining praline is delicious scattered on vanilla ice cream.

RED FRUIT CHEESECAKE

❧ SERVES 10 TO 12 • PREPARATION: 15 MINUTES • BAKING TIME: 60 MINUTES + CHILLING TIME ❧

6 ounces (175 g) digestive cookies
¼ cup (60 ml) unsalted butter
5 ounces (150 g) red fruit, plus extra to serve
1½ pounds (750 g) cream cheese
¾ cup (175 ml) buttermilk
⅓ cup (75 ml) cornstarch

Finely grated zest of 1 orange
¾ cup (175 ml) granulated or superfine sugar
2 eggs + 1 egg yolk
1 tablespoon (15 ml) vanilla extract

GARNISH:
White chocolate curls (see recipe 8)

IN ADVANCE:
Grease sides of a 9-inch (23 cm) springform pan and double-wrap it in foil. Preheat oven to 300°F (150°C).

1	Whiz the cookies in a food processor to fine crumbs.	2	Melt the butter in a pan and pour into the cookie crumbs.	3	Spread the mixture evenly over base of prepared pan and press down to get it to the sides.
4	Spread the fruit over the base and allow it to chill while making the topping.	5	Beat the remaining ingredients together until smooth and creamy.	6	Pour the cheese mix over the chilled cookie crust. ➤

7 Bake in a water bath as in recipe 62 for 1 hour. When it is ready, it should have a slight wobble. Take out of the oven and cool in the water for 45 minutes. Allow to cool in the pan, then run a knife around the edge to loosen and carefully remove the cheesecake.

TIP
❁

This is also a great recipe for summer with fresh red berries replacing the Black Forest fruits.

| 8 | Sprinkle the cheesecake with a few pieces of fruit and white chocolate curls. The cheesecake is best eaten at room temperature. | **VARIATION**
❈

Replace the red fruit with pineapple for a tropical variation, if you like. |

COCONUT & RUM CHEESECAKE

❖ SERVES 10 TO 12 • PREPARATION: 15 MINUTES • BAKING TIME: 60 MINUTES, PLUS CHILLING TIME ❖

6 ounces (175 g) digestive cookies
¼ cup (60 ml) unsalted butter
1 pound (500 g) mascarpone cheese
2 tablespoons (30 ml) cornstarch
1 cup (250 ml) heavy cream (36%)
¾ cup (175 ml) superfine raw or turbinado sugar

1 vanilla bean, seeds scraped out
2 eggs + 1 egg yolk
1 cup (250 ml) shredded coconut
2 tablespoons (30 ml) dark rum
Finely grated zest and juice of 1 lime,
  plus extra zest for topping

TOPPING:
2½-ounces (70 g) piece fresh coconut
IN ADVANCE:
Grease sides and line the base of a 9-inch
(23 cm) springform pan and double-wrap it
in foil. Preheat oven to 300°F (150°C).

1	Whiz the cookies in a food processor until they're the consistency of fine crumbs.	2	Melt the butter in a pan and pour into the crumbs.
3	Spread the mixture evenly over the bottom of the prepared pan and press down to get into edges. Chill for about 15 to 20 minutes to set.	4	Beat the mascarpone, cornstarch, cream, sugar, vanilla seeds, eggs and egg yolk until smooth and creamy. ➤

5 6
7 8

5	Add the coconut, rum, lime juice and zest into the cheese mixture and mix to combine.	6	Pour the cheese mixture over the crust. Bake in a water bath according to recipe 62 for 60 minutes. Cool in the water for 45 minutes.
7	Once the cake has cooled completely, chill for 2 hours. To take out of the pan, run a knife around the edge of the pan to loosen the cheesecake.	8	For the garnish, using a vegetable peeler, cut the fresh coconut into thin strips.

9

Scatter the coconut on top of the cheesecake, sprinkle with the lime zest and serve.

TIP

Instead of heavy cream, use canned coconut milk for extra creaminess.

RICOTTA & LEMON CHEESECAKE

❖ SERVES 10 TO 12 • PREPARATION: 35 MINUTES • BAKING TIME: 60 MINUTES ❖

7 ounces (200 g) digestive cookies
¼ cup (60 ml) unsalted butter, melted
¼ cup (60 ml) cornstarch
1¼ pounds (550 g) ricotta cheese
1¼ cups (300 ml) superfine raw or turbinado sugar
2 eggs, separated, + 1 egg yolk

¾ cup + 2 tablespoons (200 ml) heavy cream (36%)
1 tablespoon (15 ml) lemon juice
Finely grated zest of 1 lemon
GARNISH:
Confectioners' sugar, to dust

1 lemon, thinly sliced
IN ADVANCE:
Grease sides and line the base of a 9-inch (23 cm) springform cake pan and double-wrap it in foil. Preheat oven to 300°F (150°C).

1	Crush the cookies to fine crumbs in a plastic bag with a rolling pin — not too roughly as you might split the bag.	2	Melt the butter in a pan, pour into the crumbs and mix well.
3	Spread the mixture evenly over base of prepared pan and press down to get into edges. Chill for about 15 to 20 minutes to set.	4	Beat the cornstarch, ricotta cheese, sugar and all the egg yolks together until smooth and creamy. ➢

5 6
7 8

5	Whisk the egg whites in a clean bowl until stiff, then fold into the cheese mix.	6	Fold in the cream, lemon juice and zest.
7	Pour the cheese mixture over the crust and bake according to recipe 62 for 1 hour. Cool according to recipe 62.	8	Once the cake has cooled completely, run a knife around the edge to loosen it and carefully remove the cheesecake from the pan.

		TIP ❋
	Dust the cheesecake with confectioners' sugar and decorate with thin lemon slices.	This recipe also works well with oranges, using the same quantities but exchanging all the lemons with oranges.

CHOCOLATE CHEESECAKE

❦ SERVES 8 TO 10 • PREPARATION: 20 TO 25 MINUTES • CHILLING TIME: 2 TO 4 HOURS OR OVERNIGHT ❦

7 ounces (200 g) chocolate-coated cookies
¼ cup (60 ml) unsalted butter
CHEESECAKE:
5 ounces (150 g) dark chocolate, broken
  into pieces

1 teaspoon (15 ml) unflavored gelatin
2 eggs, separated
¼ cup (60 ml) granulated or superfine sugar
7ounces (225 g) cream cheese
1¼ cups (300 ml) sour cream

GARNISH:
Marbled fruits (see recipe 10)
IN ADVANCE:
Lightly grease the sides and line the base of
an 8-inch (20 cm) springform pan.

1 2
3 4

1	Whiz the cookies in a food processor until they're the consitency of fine crumbs. Melt the butter in a pan and pour into the crumbs.	2	Spread the mixture evenly over base of prepared pan and press down to get into edges. Chill for about 20 minutes to set.
3	Melt the chocolate in a heatproof bowl set over a pan of simmering water. Allow to cool slightly.	4	Put 1 tablespoon (15 ml) of water in a bowl, add the gelatin, set over a pan of simmering water and leave for 10 minutes. ➤

5	Put the egg yolks, sugar, cream cheese, sour cream and cooled chocolate in a bowl.	6	Stir the dissolved gelatin into the cheese mixture.
7	Whisk the egg whites until soft peaks form, then fold into the cheese mixture.	8	Pour the mixture over the crust and chill for 3 to 4 hours or overnight, until set.

9	Remove the cheesecake from the pan and decorate with marbled fruit.	<div align="center">TIP ❋</div>Use white chocolate instead of dark chocolate, but use 7 ounces (200 g) instead of 5 ounces (150 g).

LIGHT LEMON CHEESECAKE

❖ SERVES 10 TO 12 • PREPARATION: 45 MINUTES • CHILLING TIME: 5 TO 6 HOURS ❖

5 ounces (150 g) oatmeal cookies
¼ cup (60 ml) unsalted butter, melted
CHEESECAKE:
7 ounces (200 g) cream cheese
7 tablespoons (100 ml) unsalted butter, melted
½ cup (125 ml) granulated or superfine sugar

¼ cup (60 ml) good-quality lemon curd
3 eggs, separated
Finely grated zest of 2 lemons
Juice of 2 lemons or 5 passion fruits
2 (¼ ounce/7g) envelopes unflavored gelatin
¾ cup + 2 tablespoons (200 ml) heavy cream (36%)

GARNISH:
Lemon slices or pulp of 4 passion fruits
IN ADVANCE:
Line the base of a 9-inch (23 cm) round cake pan with a removable bottom.

1	Whiz the cookies in a food processor until fine crumbs. Melt the butter and pour into the crumbs. Press into prepared pan and chill for 20 minutes.	2	Put the cream cheese, butter, sugar, lemon curd, egg yolks, lemon zest and juice in a bowl and mix well.
3	Put 2 tablespoons (30 ml) of water in a bowl, add the gelatin, set over a pan of simmering water and leave for 10 minutes. Cool slightly.	4	Whip the cream until it is quite stiff, then fold into the cream cheese mixture along with the gelatin. ➤

	Whisk the egg whites in a clean dry bowl until stiff peaks form, then gently fold into the cream cheese mixture.	**TIP** ❋	
5		When whisking the egg whites, make sure the bowl is clean, dry and grease-free; otherwise, the egg whites will not whisk properly.	

6	Pour the mixture on top of the cookie crust. Allow to chill for 5 to 6 hours or overnight, until set. Carefully remove the cheesecake from the pan and decorate with lemon slices or passion fruit pulp.	This cheesecake also works well if lime is used instead of the lemon.

CASSIS CHEESECAKE

⇻ SERVES 10 TO 12 • PREPARATION: 30 MINUTES • CHILLING TIME: OVERNIGHT ⇺

7 ounces (200 g) shortbread
¼ cup (60 ml) unsalted butter, melted
1 pound (450 g) mixed blackberries
  and blueberries
5 tablespoons (75 ml) crème de cassis

4 (¼ ounce/7g) envelopes or 5 sheets of
  unflavored gelatin
3 tablespoons (45 ml) liquid honey
7 ounces (225 g) mascarpone cheese
⅔ cup (150 ml) sour cream
2 eggs, separated

½ cup (125 ml) granulated or superfine sugar
GARNISH:
3½ ounces (100g) blackberries
3½ ounces (100g) blueberries
IN ADVANCE: Grease the sides and line the
base of a 9-inch (23 cm) springform pan.

1	Whiz the shortbread in a food processor until fine crumbs. Pour in the butter and mix.	2	Press the mixture into base of prepared pan. Chill for about 10 minutes to set.	3	Bring the fruit and crème de cassis to a boil, then simmer for 5 minutes. Cool.
4	Dissolve the gelatin in 3 tablespoons (45 ml) of water, according to recipe 68.	5	Whiz the berries, honey, cheese, sour cream and egg yolks in a food processor until smooth. Add the gelatin.	6	Whisk egg whites until frothy. Add sugar, a spoon at a time, until stiff. ➤

| 7 | Fold the egg white mixture into the blackberry mixture, then pour over the shortbread crust. Chill overnight, until set. | **TIP**
❈
Always use a cake pan with a removable bottom for the cheesecake, as it will easier to remove the cheesecake once it is set. |

8

Run a knife (dipped in hot water) around the edges and remove the cheesecake from the pan. Decorate with blackberries and blueberries.

VARIATION

※

This is also a great recipe for summer — replace the dark purple fruit with fresh red berries.

APPENDIXES

GLOSSARY

MENUS

TABLE OF CONTENTS

RECIPE INDEX

GENERAL INDEX

ACKNOWLEDGMENTS

GLOSSARY

ALL-IN-ONE (DUMP CAKES)
Exactly as the name suggests, these cakes are mixed all in one go. All the ingredients go into the bowl together, and the mixing is done in seconds. There is no need for rubbing or creaming in this method and no danger of the cake curdling because of the egg being added too quickly. The fat must always be very soft for this method.

BEAT
To thoroughly combine ingredients and incorporate air with a rapid, circular motion. This may be done with a wire whisk, electric mixer or food processor.

BUTTER
Unless otherwise stated, should be unsalted and left at room temperature for at least 30 minutes to soften. Even then, sometimes it is best to cream the butter alone before adding the sugar.

CARAMEL
The French term for browned sugar. In its most basic form, caramel is made by heating sugar and water, at which point it takes on varying degrees of color and obtains its distinctive taste. If cooked too long, it darkens and turns bitter.

CREAM
To soften solid fats (i.e., butter), working with a wooden spoon or electric mixer until the fat is creamy and then adding sugar and beating until the mixture is pale and fluffy. In a creamed mixture, eggs are gradually beaten in and the flour is carefully folded into the creamed mixture. The eggs must always be at room temperature and be added one at a time and mixed in thoroughly after each egg to avoid curdling. To also prevent curdling, a spoonful of sifted flour may be added with each egg addition. However, the remaining flour still needs to be very lightly folded in.

DOUBLE-BOILER
A two-pan or pan-and-bowl system with a pan of water that is used to help mixtures such as chocolate melt and to protect them from the direct heat of the stove.

DUST
To lightly sprinkle the surface of the cake with confectioners' sugar or other garnish, such as edible glitter.

FOLD
To incorporate a delicate mixture into a thicker, heavier mixture with a large metal spoon or rubber spatula without stirring, so that the finished product remains very light.

FRUIT
Either dried or fresh, fruit adds flavor and moisture to cakes. Dried fruits are usually washed and ready to use, but try to get the best quality as they are usually moister and better tasting. When storing dried fruit, ensure that no air can get to it, as the air will dry out the fruit and alter its taste. Fresh fruits always add character to a cake but must be of the freshest and best quality. Try to use the best seasonal fruit when available. However, suitable replacements can always be found. For example, the peach upside-down cake works just as well with apricots.

GREASE
To lightly rub fat on the surface of a baking pan.

LINE
Use parchment paper to line the base of your non-stick baking pan. To make a good fit, place the pan on top of the paper, trace around the pan and cut it out, just inside the marked circle. Fit it to an already greased pan.

MEASURING SPOONS
Are used for measuring out smaller amounts. A set of accurate measuring spoons is vital. Always try to get the best-quality ones available. The amounts given in this book are always based upon level spoonfuls.

MELTING
Melting butter before adding to a cake mixture makes the cake moister and changes the texture when carried out correctly. It is best to melt the butter in a small pan on the stove, making sure that it doesn't bubble. Once removed from the heat, the butter must be cooled a little before adding to the cake — if still hot, it will cook the flour, resulting in a tough cake.

MIX
To stir together two or more ingredients until they are thoroughly combined.

PALETTE KNIFE
A long, thin metal spatula used for decorating cakes. They come in a variety of sizes and are very useful for spreading fillings and toppings smoothly.

PANS
Non-stick pans are an asset, though well-greased metal cake pans will generally suffice. Layer cake pans are usually shallow — about 1½ inches (4 cm) deep — but some recipes, such as the blood orange and almond cake (recipe 24), require a pan that is 3 inches (7.5 cm) deep. Standard loaf pans are about 8 by 4 inches (20 by 10 cm) and 9 by 5

inches (23 by 13 cm). Pans with a removable bottom and either rigid or hinged (springform) sides facilitate removal. And cake molds come in various sizes and shapes. Tube, Bundt and kugelhopf molds are most widely available.

SCALES
Used to accurately record the weight of ingredients. Scales are particularly important for consistent baking results. They come in a variety of shapes and sizes. There are electric and manual scales. Since digital scales are extremely accurate and low in cost, it's highly recommend you buy these for better results.

SEPARATE THE EGG (EGGS)
To remove the yolk from the white of an egg.

SIFT
To sift flour or dry ingredients through a sieve, which removes any lumps and gives a light dusting effect. Sifting incorporates air into the flour.

SOFT PEAKS
When egg whites or whipping cream is beaten until the peaks are rounded or curl when beaters are lifted from the bowl while still being moist and glossy.

STIFF PEAKS
To beat egg whites to the stage where the mixture will hold stiff, pointed peaks when the beaters are removed.

STORAGE
The method of preserving the cake for later consumption. Many methods of storage can be used, from plastic wrap to large containers. Depending on the shape and size of the cake, the aim is to not let air get to the cake so as to retain the moisture. Plastic wrap or aluminum foil are both very good for smaller cakes with little or no decoration. Freezer bags have a similar function and are essential when freezing cakes. For larger cakes, plastic containers that are airtight are a good solution, as well as some large round cookie tins. The cake can be placed on top of the lid and then the other part of the tin/container can be placed on top, which makes for easier removal.

VANILLA BEANS
The pods can be used either whole or split to reveal the aromatic seeds, which can be scraped out and added to cakes or custards.

VANILLA EXTRACT
Vanilla extract is an alcoholic solution with the true flavor and aroma of vanilla beans. Those labeled "pure vanilla extract" are the best quality. Vanilla extract can be used as flavoring in place of the real thing, but avoid using products labeled "vanilla flavoring," which lack the true flavor and aroma of vanilla.

WATER BATH (BAIN-MARIE)
A large dish (such as a roasting pan) that is partially filled with water, into which cakes are placed. It is used to protect the cakes from the direct heat of the oven.

WHIP
To beat quickly and steadily by hand with a whisk or electric mixer.

WHISKING
A technique (using either a handheld electric beater or a balloon whisk) used for beating the sugar and eggs into a thick mix. Also used for beating egg whites into a soft light foam, especially for use with light sponges, where the cake rises due to the air that is incorporated during the whisking of the eggs.

WIRE RACKS
An essential item for the cooling of cakes. Many shapes and sizes are available. Large rectangular racks are particularly good when cooling one or more cakes, and of course the rack from your broiler or roasting pan can also provide a good wire rack.

ZEST
The colored outer peel of citrus fruit, which is used to add flavor. The zest is often referred to as grated peel in recipes. To create zest, choose the diagonal-hole side of a box grater, as it will give you a cleaner zesting than the nail-hole side, or a Microplane grater. Rub lightly to avoid getting the white pith, which is bitter.

MENUS

~~~~~~~~~~~~~~~~~~~~

AFTERNOON TEA PARTY

KID'S PARTY

GIRLS' NIGHT IN PARTY

BABY SHOWER

IMPRESS THE IN-LAWS

SUMMER PICNIC

QUICK & EASY

TABLE OF CONTENTS

1

BASICS

2

SIMPLE CAKES

3

LAYER CAKES

4

LOAF CAKES

5

CHOCOLATE CAKES

6

CHEESECAKES

RECIPE INDEX

INGREDIENTS

DEDICATION

To Mom and Dad for all your love and support.

ACKNOWLEDGMENTS

My thanks to my amazing family for their love,
support and help over the years: to Ben, Kirsty, Daniel, Rosea,
Samuel, Rachel, Nathan, Naomi, Hanna, Jacob and to Auntie Anne and Zak and family.

Big thanks to Rebecca Fawcett for all her help and support.
To Kate McCullough and Yasmin Othman, for all their help on the shoot,
long live all the yummy cakes! Thanks go to Deirdre Rooney for all the amazing photographs.
Thanks also to Catie Ziller, Sarah Tildesley and to Kathy Steer for her wonderful editorial work.

And thanks to all those who have helped me along the way;
Anna J, Anna H, Anthony, Chrispana, Colette, Emily, Fions, Gary,
Ginny, Georgie, Karen, Lisa, Paul R, Ruth, Sole and to Danni for all those
years ago making cakes on a Saturday afternoon.

3309707062745